About the author

Aggie MacKenzie has worked on a number of national magazines, and was associate editor in charge of the Good Housekeeping Institute. Her current work covers a variety of areas – aside from co-presenting *How Clean Is Your House?*, she writes a column for *The Times*, frequently partakes in advertising campaigns and has appeared on many different programmes including *Market Kitchen*, *The One Show* and *Dancing On Ice*. Aggie is married, has two sons and lives in north London. When Aggie's not working, cleaning or tending to her allotment she loves to cook.

Ask Aggie

For All Your Cleaning Solutions

Aggie MacKenzie
with Emma Burton

MICHAEL JOSEPH
an imprint of
PENGUIN BOOKS

PENGUIN BOOKS

Published by the Penguin Group

Penguin Books Ltd, 80 Strand, London WC2R 0RL, England

Penguin Group (USA) Inc., 375 Hudson Street, New York, New York 10014, USA

Penguin Group (Canada), 90 Eglinton Avenue East, Suite 700, Toronto, Ontario,
Canada M4P 2Y3 (a division of Pearson Penguin Canada Inc.)

Penguin Ireland, 25 St Stephen's Green, Dublin 2, Ireland (a division of Penguin Books Ltd)

Penguin Group (Australia), 250 Camberwell Road, Camberwell, Victoria 3124, Australia
(a division of Pearson Australia Group Pty Ltd)

Penguin Books India Pvt Ltd, 11 Community Centre, Panchsheel Park,
New Delhi – 110 017, India

Penguin Group (NZ), 67 Apollo Drive, Rosedale, North Shore 0632, New Zealand
(a division of Pearson New Zealand Ltd)

Penguin Books (South Africa) (Pty) Ltd, 24 Sturdee Avenue, Rosebank,
Johannesburg 2196, South Africa

Penguin Books Ltd, Registered Offices: 80 Strand, London WC2R 0RL, England

www.penguin.com

First published 2009

Columns originally published in *The Times*, 2004–2008

5

Copyright © Aggie MacKenzie, 2009
All rights reserved

The moral right of the author has been asserted

Designed and set by seagulls.net
Printed in England by Clays Ltd, St Ives plc

ISBN: 978–0–141–04281–7

www.greenpenguin.co.uk

Mixed Sources
Product group from well-managed
forests and other controlled sources
www.fsc.org Cert no. SA-COC-1592
© 1996 Forest Stewardship Council

Penguin Books is committed to a sustainable future
for our business, our readers and our planet.
The book in your hands is made from paper
certified by the Forest Stewardship Council.

For Matthew, a true friend

Contents

All prices listed were correct on date of publication.

Introduction

I've lost count of the number of times I've been asked, 'How do you know all this stuff?' Truth is, one way or another I've been sort of living the domestic life for nigh-on 50 years. My household knowledge came first from my mother, that's for sure. In her late teens she went from the remote northwest of Scotland to work in service in a large London residence – at the Air Minister's in Kensington, no less – and quickly learned the proper way to carry out domestic duties. As I and my three sisters were growing up, we had no option but to be drilled in the correct way to sweep a floor, form a hospital corner and polish a sideboard.

Now a mother of two teenage boys myself, I hear my own mother's voice as I yell, 'Can you please *not* rub the whole of your grubby palm against the white wall as you come downstairs?' It's definitely a generation thing.

Over the past 30 years I've done time on a succession of women's magazines, always picking up domestic hints and tips along the way. Latterly I was at *Good Housekeeping*, overseeing the consumer and cookery departments, whose expert teams are walking, talking aficionados in all matters domestic. Indeed, each January we used to run a 'Stains Special' feature in the magazine, which was hugely popular with the readers.

Towards the end of 2002 I successfully auditioned to co-present a new Channel 4 programme, and *How Clean Is Your House?* was born. A year later I was asked both to commit to another TV series and to write a weekly column, 'Ask Aggie', for *The Times*. Life was changing fast and time constraints meant I had to leave my job and friends at *Good Housekeeping*.

For a few years now the other question I'm often asked by *Times* readers is: 'Will there be a book of all your advice?' So I am glad to say that, at last, here it is. Please note that because all the queries are genuine questions put to me by readers over the past five years (as opposed to rewritten press puffs), it's an intriguing, eclectic mix, and sorting the chapters hasn't been the easiest job. But here it is: a collection of real domestic problems from real readers, as organised as it can be, with a comprehensive index, and I do hope it will be of great help to you.

It's a source of amazement to me that there seems to be no end to new questions that need answers, and with this in mind you're very welcome to write to me at aggie.mackenzie@thetimes.co.uk. Happy homemaking!

Questions I'm forever being asked

1 There's black gunk round the seal of my washing machine – how to get rid? (page 99)

2 What's the secret of hotel-fluffy towels? (page 76)

3 Someone's put a cup of coffee on my polished table and it's left a mark. Help! (page 104)

4 What's an easy way to get rid of limescale on taps? (page 65)

5 Watermarks on my showerscreen are driving me mad – what to do? (page 59)

6 How do I get greying whites white again? (page 89)

7 What's the answer to glasses that have become cloudy from dishwasher use? (page 15)

8 When I got my son's old christening robe out of the cupboard for my grandson, it had yellowed. How can I get it white again? (page 90)

9 My shower curtain gets mouldy stains at the base. What's the easy answer? (page 55)

10 How do I remove fly spots baked hard on to the surface of a fabric lampshade? (page 149)

10 common stains — and how to magic them away

1 Biro on clothes (page 82)

2 Sunscreen on clothes (page 81)

3 Sweat marks on shirt armpits (page 75)

4 Rust-like marks on washing (page 98)

5 Vomit/urine/blood on mattress (page 174)

6 Lily pollen on clothes (page 74)

7 Blu-Tack on painted wall (page 184) and carpets (page 122)

8 Colour-run accidents in washing machine (page 97)

9 Mystery marks on enamel bath/lavatory bowl (pages 62 and 68)

10 Grease on headboard/sofa (page 104)

Pesky household pests & how to show them the door

1 Clothes moths (page 147)

2 Flour moths (page 157)

3 Mice (page 156)

4 Ants (page 149)

5 Woodlice (page 150)

6 Woolly bears (page 151)

7 Silverfish (page 155)

8 Dust mites (page 153)

9 Flies (page 156)

10 Bed bugs (page 154)

Bad smells – and how to zap them

1 The washing machine gives off a nasty odour (page 99)

2 My son's trainers are beyond the pale (page 160)

3 I burned a ready meal in the microwave weeks ago and the smell persists (page 26)

4 My cat wees persistently and I cannot get rid of the nasty niff completely (page 144)

5 I got back from holiday to find the fridge-freezer fuse had blown in my absence. It works again, and has been cleaned, but still stinks (page 27)

6 I've scrubbed my newly bought Victorian pine chest of drawers but the mothball smell won't go away (page 109)

7 My shirts give off a sweaty smell when I iron (page 96)

8 I've inherited some valuable antique books that smell musty (page 160)

9 The waste disposal unit gives off a drainy stench (page 25)

10 I want to use my vacuum flask for cold drinks in the summer, but it smells strongly of coffee (page 46)

Thank God for dirty dishes,
They have a tale to tell;
While others may go hungry,
We're eating very well
_____

Anon

Kitchen

Q I live in a hard-water area and the inside of my kettle is caked in limescale. What's the best way to deal with it?

A Fill the kettle with half water, half clear vinegar, taking the solution just over the scale line, and bring just to the boil. Switch off and leave to cool until the fizzing stops. Leave overnight if the limescale is really caked on. Shift stubborn deposits with a nylon brush and re-boil if necessary. Flush well with lots of clean water before you make your next brew. Repeat every few months, depending on how hard your water is.

Q Why does the dishwasher make my glasses cloudy? How can I get rid of the film, and stop it happening if I buy new ones?

A There are a few possible reasons for this. First, you may not be using enough salt, which is causing hard-water deposits to build up, especially if you live in a hard-water area. Or you're overdosing with rinse aid. Re-wash the glasses in the dishwasher, making sure the rinse aid and salt levels are topped up and dosing correctly, and that you're using the right amount of detergent. No difference? Then fill the detergent dispenser with Dri-Pak citric acid powder, from hardware stores, and run the glasses through a normal wash without detergent. The citric acid acts as a limescale remover, so even if your glasses are past it and the bloom remains, at least you'll have descaled the dishwasher.

The high wash temperatures and detergent inside the dishwasher can also attack the glass, giving it a cloudy appearance. Depending on the glass quality, this can happen after just a few or a lot of washes, or might never occur, but if it does, no amount of scrubbing will sort it.

Scratch marks can also build up on glasses where they've rubbed against each other during the wash. These can appear as a cloudy ring and usually occur at the widest part of the glass. Again, this mechanical scratching is permanent, so always make sure you leave space between items when loading the dishwasher.

Finally, white spots can appear on glasses, making them look dirty and dull. This is usually caused by detergent residues or water droplets drying on the surface. Always use a rinse aid and check detergent dosage.

But the hard truth is that if you want your glasses to stay sparklingly clear, you need to wash them by hand. (At least your good ones. You can buy dishwasher-safe glasses that are less susceptible to dishwasher damage, but even these will eventually go cloudy over time: wash on a short, low temperature cycle and use a detergent with glass protection.) When handwashing glasses, use hot soapy water first, then rinse with very hot water from the tap. Dry immediately with a clean, soft, linen tea towel and they'll sparkle beautifully.

Q **When I unload my dishwasher I often find gritty silt stuck on to the crockery and inside the glasses. What's happening?**

A You're not alone. This is caused by food residues being re-deposited on to items during the wash. Follow these tips:

✳ Scrape plates before loading.

✳ Load items so that water can get to every surface.

✳ Make sure the inlet pipe for the top spray arm isn't covered.

✳ Don't overload – squeezing in those extra bits never works.

✳ Wash cutlery with handles down (except sharp knives).

✳ Make sure spray arms can rotate freely.

✳ Use a pre-wash for heavily soiled loads.

✳ Empty filters after every few washes and regularly clean in hot soapy water.

✳ Clean spray arms regularly in a solution of washing-up liquid – use a needle to poke out any limescale and run water through the inlet of each spray arm to check that holes aren't blocked with food debris.

✳ Use the correct amount of detergent.

✳ Make sure salt and rinse aid levels are always topped up.

✳ Still no joy? Call in an engineer.

Q I'm confused by those dishwasher tablets with built-in rinse aid and salt. Do I still need to add these products separately?

A Unless you live in an extremely hard-water area, you don't need extra rinse aid or salt on top of the all-in-one tablets.

Hard water is over 26 degrees Clarke, expressed as 26e, or 370 parts per million of calcium carbonate, the stuff that makes water hard. To check your water hardness, contact your supplier – most have a website and are in the phone book. To convert parts per million (ppm) to degrees Clarke (e), use the following formula: $1ppm = 0.07e$.

According to the makers, all-in-one tablets have enough of both rinse aid and salt for each wash, and work in soft, medium and hard water (up to the magic 26e level), even if the rinse aid or salt warning lights come on. However, you may need to add a little extra rinse aid for a squeaky-clean finish. If your water is over 26e, it's cheaper to use the standard tablets and add your own salt and rinse aid.

Q I was given four crystal glasses in the 1970s which have gone milky through dishwasher use. I've tried cleaning them with vinegar, lemon juice and bicarbonate of soda, without success. Would anything else work?

A You shouldn't really put lead crystal in the dishwasher. Apart from the cost of replacing it if it gets chipped, the high lead content makes the glass very soft and susceptible to dishwasher damage (which is why it's easy to engrave). The hot wash temperatures and detergent attack the glass, giving it a milky bloom. This can happen after just a few washes, and no amount of scrubbing will sort it. (You should take care with plain glass, as well: wash in the dishwasher on a short, low temperature cycle using a detergent with glass protection, as it too will eventually go cloudy.)

But here's the good news: for around £4 a glass (plus p&p) you can get them re-dipped in acid to remove the bloom and restore the sparkle. You won't get that just-new shine, however, and it can highlight any scratches and remove engraving. Contact Redhouse Glass Crafts on 01384 399460. Send your glasses by special delivery in plenty of bubble-wrap, newspaper or polystyrene chippings, and enclose a covering letter. Allow up to 10 days.

Otherwise, you might want to replace them with lead-free crystal ones. Instead of lead, they contain other metals to give the glass clarity and weight, making them more hardwearing. However, although they're less susceptible (compared with lead crystal) to dishwasher damage, they can, like plain glass, eventually go cloudy too. But they are cheaper to replace at around a third of the price of lead crystal. Dartington Crystal does a lead-free crystal range called Wine Debut, £28 for a set of four glasses. Contact 01805 626262 or order online at www.dartington.co.uk; add £8 p&p.

Q Is there an eco-friendly way of de-scaling the water jets on my dishwasher?

A There is, and even if you don't live in a hard-water area, it's worth reading this, since not only limescale but also bits of food can get clogged in the spray arm jets and reduce wash performance, so it's a good idea to check and clean them every few months.

Most spray arms can be unscrewed and removed from the dishwasher for easier cleaning (check the instructions if you're not sure). Wash them in hot soapy water and give them a good scrub with a nylon brush. Use a needle to poke out any stubborn debris and run hot water through the inlet of each spray arm to ensure that holes aren't blocked. Replace the arms and check that they rotate freely. While you're at it, run a cupful of clear vinegar through a cycle of the dishwasher (empty and without detergent) to remove grease and limescale and leave it clean and fresh. It's a good idea to wipe around the door seals and hinges with vinegar too. Finally, remove the filter regularly and clean it with hot soapy water.

Q After removing the packaging on my new stainless-steel dishwasher, I discovered a huge sticker in the middle of the door. I tried to peel it off, but the glue was strong and, since then, I have been unable to remove any more than the surface paper. I have tried soapy water and a microfibre cloth, but with no luck. What should I do next?

TOP TIP
How to stop your dishwasher smelling...

Your dishwasher quickly gathers grease and limescale, which builds up in the pipes, spray arms and filters. If it's not dealt with, your dishwasher will become less efficient and get smelly. To get rid of this build-up, either run a cup of clear vinegar through the cycle when the dishwasher is empty, or use Finish Dishwasher Cleaner, from supermarkets. It's a good idea, too, to wipe around the door seals and hinges with the solution. Clean the filters every day or so in hot soapy water, check the spray arms for food debris and clean them regularly, and use the right amount of detergent for your wash cycle.

One last tip to banish smells: sprinkle a couple of tablespoons of bicarbonate of soda on the bottom of the dishwasher, or put half a lemon on the top rack before running a load.

A Spray the area with WD-40 and leave it for 30 seconds, then give it a wipe and the sticky residue will dissolve before your eyes (you might have to spray a few times). If there are any stubborn marks remaining, gently take a plastic scraper to them. Finish by washing down the door with warm soapy water and buff dry.

Q How do I clean my deep fat fryer? It's non-stick on the inside and stainless steel and plastic outside. And what am I supposed to do with the old oil?

A It seems that no matter how you treat it, a deep fat fryer always ends up a horrible sticky mess. But here are some tips.

* Always give the inside a good clean every time the oil is changed – usually every four to six uses.

* Some fryers have a removable bowl, basket and lid that can be washed in the dishwasher, but check the instructions.

* Treat baked-on grease with washing soda. Sprinkle a cup of crystals into a pint of hot water and leave to soak overnight. Rinse well, scrubbing with a nylon scourer to loosen stubborn bits. (Take care not to damage the non-stick coating.)

* Alternatively, make up a solution of hot water and washing detergent (a couple of tablespoons or a tablet to a pint of water, but it must be biological detergent to break down the grease).

* Wipe the outside with a damp cloth and non-abrasive cleaner.

* For the old oil, soak up small quantities with kitchen towel or newspaper, then discard it in your normal rubbish (or organic waste recycling bin if you have one). But for larger quantities, you must take the oil in bottles to your local authority waste disposal site.

Q Our much-loved Magimix juice extractor is used solely for our morning vegetable juice and it shows,

with staining both on the metal extractor and the plastic. What can we do to sort it out?

A A bit late now, I know, but the secret is to remove the pulp and wash all the removable parts immediately after use, as the pulp is difficult to deal with if left to dry (soak the filter in hot soapy water to soften any stubborn hardened bits). Your Magimix lid and bowl are dishwasher safe (top rack only), which will make things a bit easier, otherwise wash them by hand and scrub with a nylon brush under running water.

Try the following tips to deal with the extractor's discoloured parts. Wipe with kitchen paper moistened with vegetable oil, then wash in hot soapy water. Or you could use lemon juice, which is a natural bleaching agent; leave a few minutes before washing it off. Alternatively, soak it in a solution of Milton Sterilising Fluid, from supermarkets (dilute according to the instructions).

Q My wife gave me an espresso coffee machine for my birthday, which makes wonderful coffee. But however hard I try, I'm having trouble keeping the holes in the filter clean. What should I do?

A Hard water is probably the problem. The holes in the filter are so tiny they easily clog up with limescale. You've probably noticed that this has affected the flow and it takes ages to make your coffee. You need to de-scale the filter regularly – every two to three weeks – by soaking it in neat lemon juice or a vinegar solution (one part clear vinegar to two parts water). Rinse and dry well. For daily cleaning, just rinse under the tap.

Another thought: you may be using too fine a coffee. The filter will get clogged if the grains are over-fine, which will affect the flow and make cleaning harder. Always use a medium-ground espresso coffee – harder to gauge if you grind your own, but keep practising!

Q The inside of my Italian espresso coffee maker (made of aluminium alloy, its upper and lower parts screwing together with the ground coffee sitting in the middle) has become blackened. What's the best cleaning method?
A Worry not – the staining is actually a good thing! It helps to protect the coffee from the metal surface and improves the flavour as there's no metallic aftertaste. In fact, when you buy a new aluminium stove-top coffee maker you should always boil some plain water through several times before using it. This creates a lining of limescale which will prevent the coffee taking on a metallic taste. (Do this even if you live in a soft-water area, as you'll be building up some deposits.) Just rinse out the coffee maker with plain water after each use and store the parts separately to allow the air to flow through freely.

The only time you need to clean the inside is if any mould forms: if it does, wash it in hot soapy water using a hard nylon brush (an old toothbrush is great for getting into the corners). Rinse well, then boil some water through, without coffee, to sterilise. But remember, you'll need to repeat the pre-boiling process before using the pot again.

If the blackness still bothers you, ditch the aluminium coffee maker in favour of a stainless steel version. Stainless steel is inert and the surface impenetrable, so you won't have to do the pre-boiling stage, as there's no problem with the metal tainting the coffee. It won't get stained, either, if you rinse it out after every use.

Q How can I remove the green bloom on the inside of the clear plastic water level tube of my coffee maker? It's resisted all attempts at cleaning and de-scaling, and really bothers me as I use the machine daily.
A It's probably mould. Try filling the water tank with a solution of Milton Sterilising Fluid (dilute according to the instructions), making sure it completely covers the stained area. Leave to stand overnight (don't switch on the machine) and then flush with plenty of clean water. This will help kill any bacteria and sterilise the tube, but to avoid it happening again, always make sure the tank is empty after you've used the machine.

Q My kitchen waste disposal unit smells quite nasty at times. What should I do?
A Quarter a lemon and whizz it in the unit with lots of water. Or use a bicarbonate of soda solution (one tablespoon to a pint of hot water). If that doesn't work, try adding a few small

chicken bones to act as an abrasive to scour the inside of the grinding chamber – it's a good idea to do this every now and again to keep the unit clean. (Most units take bones, but check the instructions.)

Follow with a diluted bleach solution – don't use drain cleaners as these might damage the unit. You can chuck in almost all your food scraps except fruit stones, raw chicken skin (too rubbery), rhubarb and celery (too stringy). It shouldn't smell as long as you use plenty of water during and for a few seconds after grinding to flush everything through. If you don't run enough water, pipes can get blocked. You only get smells when you leave food in the unit for some time, so empty it before you go away!

Q I was defrosting a naan bread in my microwave … and forgot about it. The naan blackened and the smell was unbelievable. After three weeks, the stench persists and the microwave has now been banished to the patio. I can't be the first person to have burned something that needed only seconds. What should I do?

A The problem is that the smell gets right inside the microwave: wiping the cavity won't cut it, you'll need to clean the vents as well. To do this, put a few slices of lemon in a bowl of hot water and heat in the microwave, uncovered, on high for about ten minutes. The fragrant steam will pass through the vents and extinguish the lingering odours. Expect to have to do this a few times before you notice any improvement, but persevere; the smell will go eventually. (Don't be tempted to shortcut with something stronger, such as eucalyptus oil – it'll give your food a disgusting taste.) When the smell has gone, wipe the inside of the oven with a warm, mild solution of washing-up liquid, then dry it with paper towel. Also, leave the door open when the oven's not in use to allow the air to circulate. By the way, if you think the naan may have caught fire, you should get an engineer to check that the internal workings haven't been damaged.

Q We've just returned from holiday to a switched-off freezer containing two-week-old defrosted raw meat. How can we get rid of the stench?
A Once the smell is in the plastic it's difficult to shift. Try smearing a paste of bicarbonate of soda on the inside. Quantities aren't crucial – aim for the consistency of toothpaste and leave it, with a bowl of hot water and cut lemons (keep refilling with hot water), for 24 hours with the freezer door open. Rinse off thoroughly, give the walls a thorough wipe-down with Milton Sterilising Fluid, paying particular attention to door seals, and allow to air-dry. Wash the drawers in warm soapy water.

If it's frost-free, there'll be an evaporator tray at the back, and if it's accessible, a drainage gulley and hole inside the freezer. Blood will have got inside these, so if you can see a drainage hole, clean it by pouring a solution of the Milton down the hole to sterilise the tubes. Dilute according to the instructions, and use about a quarter of a teacupful. Then pull

out the freezer and use the Milton to clean out any contami-
nated defrost water in the evaporator tray at the back (the heat
from the compressor can worsen smells).

I'm afraid if none of this works, it's time to ditch the freezer
(check your insurance policy to see if you're covered).

**Q We have two fridges and two freezers and the door
seals on all have become black. Household cleaners
haven't made a whit of difference and we've been told by
the suppliers we need to buy new doors as the seals are
not replaceable. Is there any way of cleaning them?**
A Try Milton Sterilising Fluid. The black marks are mould
spores and if you use ordinary cleaners, they will survive and
carry on multiplying. Dilute the fluid according to instructions
and wipe the seals, paying attention to the folds, and allow to
air-dry – no need to rinse. Repeat every month or so. If this
doesn't work, maybe it *is* time to replace the doors as the seals
may be starting to perish. Or perhaps the room where the
appliances are stored is damp?

**Q Is nothing built to last these days? Our new fridge-
freezer already has a couple of unsightly scratches – the
white finish seems paper-thin. These scratches are an inch
long and the thickness of thread. What's the best way to
hide them?**
A Spray them with a couple of coats of Plasti-kote Appliance
Spray, from DIY or hardware stores, or contact 01223

836400; www.plasti-kote.com for stockists. Although it's an enamel spray paint, the manufacturer claims it gives a long-lasting finish that won't turn yellow. The spray is touch-dry in under an hour. It comes in two colours: satin chrome and gloss white. For best results, make sure the surface is clean and dry, then spray lightly – several thin coats are better than one heavy spray. Practise on a cardboard box to perfect your technique. For deep scratches – where you can see the bare metal under-neath – you should first apply Plasti-Kote's Metal Primer for rust protection (stockists as before). And no shortcuts: protect the floor and nearby surfaces before you begin and make sure the room is well ventilated.

Q I have an old double-size Breville sandwich maker that I don't use very often. I've never cleaned it and although it now smokes badly when I use it, it still works well. How should I clean it?

A I have resolved not to be judgemental and say how unsavoury that sounds. Heat the machine for a few minutes, unplug and allow it to cool slightly, then clean gently while still warm with warm soapy water and a soft cloth. This will help soften any hardened food residues and make them easier to remove. Avoid abrasives, as these will scratch any non-stick surface, and never use anything stronger than washing-up liquid, otherwise it could taint the food. Then – and don't faint at this – get into the habit of cleaning it after every use – a wipe with a damp cloth is all you need. Make sure you butter the bread well, place it on the *outside* of your toastie (to reduce sticking) and don't over-fill.

If it still smokes, why not treat yourself to a new one, preferably with removable plates that can be put into the dishwasher?

★ TOP TIP ★

How to clean a greasy oven when the interior glass has baked-on marks...

Isn't it the worst job ever? Little wonder that so many of us put it off for so long and then it turns into an even bigger bore. Here are a few trade secrets.

Place an ovenproof bowl of water in the oven at a high temperature for half an hour. The steam will soften the dirt, making it easier to remove. Then get to work with something like Mr Muscle Oven Cleaner, making sure it doesn't come into contact with any self-clean linings (which are rough to the touch). Wear rubber gloves and ventilate the room well. Cover the floor with newspaper to absorb spillages.

The secret weapon in this process is a glass scraper – like the sort used for paint splashes on windows. Use it to shift the grot from glass oven doors and floors. If the glass is removable, unscrew it, soak in a hot solution of biological washing powder, then scrape to remove stuck-on bits.

Clean racks in the dishwasher. Remove before the

---

drying cycle and chip off the residue with the back of a knife. Or soak them instead in a hot solution of biological washing powder (in the bath if the sink's too small, but protect the surface with a towel).

If this sounds too much of a faff, use Oven Pride, from supermarkets. The kit includes cleaning solution, disposable gloves and a bag for your racks and glass door (if removable). Place them in the bag, add some of the solution and seal. Take outside to avoid damage to surfaces. Leave four or five hours (ideally overnight) and work the solution over the racks every now and again to ensure deposits are coated. Wash in hot soapy water (you may have to scrub a little). The residue can be tipped down the sink and the bag thrown away.

The rest of the solution can be smeared on the oven interior with a nylon brush (not on self-clean linings, remember). It's thick enough to cling to the sides, but it's still messy. Doesn't smell bad, though! Leave this for at least four hours (ideally overnight), then wash off with hot soapy water.

After cleaning, smear a thin paste of bicarbonate of soda and water on enamel linings (except self-clean linings). This dries to leave a protective layer that absorbs greasy soiling and makes it easier to clean the oven next time. It looks messy but it works very well.

Q The instructions on my George Foreman Grill say to allow the plates to cool before cleaning, but by that time everything is stuck on. Is there an easy way to clean them?

A Actually it's fine to clean the plates while they're still warm and before everything goes rigid. After using, unplug and allow to cool slightly, then clean with warm soapy water and a soft cloth (use the spatula supplied with the grill to get into the grooves). Or you can buy George Foreman Grill sponges with non-stick scourers, which are shaped to fit into the grooves – call 0845 6589700 for stockists or buy online at www.george-foremangrills.co.uk). If this still isn't cutting it, dip a cloth into lemon juice and salt and gently rub over the surface: the lemon will cut through the grease, and the salt will act as a mild abrasive. But don't use anything rougher as it could scratch the non-stick surface. Rinse with a clean cloth.

Q How can I clean the metal grilles in my cooker hood? However much I scrub, they always feel greasy.

A Most can go in the dishwasher, so if you have one, put the grilles in on a hot wash. If not, give them a good long soak in a hot, strong solution of washing soda – about one cupful of crystals to a pint of hot water – and leave overnight. If the grilles are too big to fit in the sink, stick them in the bath instead (line with a towel to avoid scratches). Still greasy after all that? Refresh the hot-water solution and get the last of the gunk off with a nylon brush, then rinse and dry well.

Q I have a stainless-steel cooker hood that always looks greasy. A friend suggested baby oil, but grease lies on top of the oil and the only way I can get it off is with turps, which smells nasty. What can I do?

A Well, I'd forget the baby oil. Instead, start by giving the hood a deep clean with either Cif or a strong solution of washing-up liquid. From now on, use the E-Cloth Kitchen Pack, from B&Q, John Lewis, Lakeland, Robert Dyas or Waitrose. It contains two microfibre cloths: one for cleaning, the other for buffing to a shine. No need for detergents; just use water (amazingly, it does cut through the grease). The cloths can be machine washed up to 90°C and last for ages.

Q How do I clean fat deposits from electric sockets without giving myself a shock?

A Sounds obvious, but first unplug appliances and switch off the electricity supply at the mains. Then wipe the socket with a barely damp cloth rinsed in a hot, strong washing-up solution. For stubborn marks, use a plastic scourer; this may scratch, so rub in a circular motion to blend the scrubbed area into the surrounding surface. Rinse with a clean, barely damp cloth, and dry with kitchen paper before switching the electricity back on.

Q I was boiling bones for stock with the extractor fan running, but the pan boiled dry and there was lots of smoke. The hood's motor and fan still smell awful, even though I've washed the filter. Can you help?

A It sounds as if some smoke-filled grease particles have managed to get past the filters through to the motor or inside the ducting hose. A couple of suggestions (turn off at the mains first): drop the motor from its housing and give it a good wipe-down with hot soapy water. Don't overwet, and dry thoroughly before replacing. If you're not happy about doing this yourself, get a kitchen fitter in. Clean or replace the ducting hose. Washing it (in hot soapy water) is not the most pleasant task, so you may want to replace it. Again, you might be able to do it yourself (it simply unclips), depending on how · it's fitted; otherwise, contact the manufacturer or a kitchen fitter. Afterwards, wash the filter monthly (the metal mesh type are usually dishwasher safe, but for baked-on grease, soak overnight in a washing-soda solution, then wash again). Regularly wipe around the inside of the unit. Finally, to stop smells lingering after cooking, switch on the hood 10 minutes before you start and run for a few minutes afterwards.

Q We moved house recently and after only a few months the metal hobs of the electric cooker are black with burnt-on food. I've tried scrubbing with scourers and kitchen cleaners but with no luck. Please help – it looks disgusting.

A I'm assuming your hob has sealed plates, which aren't the easiest to clean. Depending on how encrusted they are, you might have to settle for a less-than-perfect finish. Make sure the plates are turned off and cool, and then clean using a nylon scourer and Bar Keepers Friend, from supermarkets. Mix with a little water and apply the paste, rubbing in a circular pattern and following the grooves on the hob plates. Take care on the metal trims to avoid scratches. Rinse and dry thoroughly. Get into the habit of wiping down the hob with a damp cloth after every use, to keep burnt-on deposits to a minimum.

Q I accidentally put a plastic food pack on a burner on my ceramic hob while it was switched on and the pack melted. Some of the burnt-on plastic came off when the burner cooled and a bit more when I used a hob cleaner and a manufacturer's razor, but there are still traces left. What should I do?

A You've done all the right things but I wonder which hob scraper you're using? A good choice is Homecare's ceramic hob scraper sold as part of their Hob Brite Accessory Kit from John Lewis, Lakeland and Robert Dyas. Its flexible stainless-steel blade can shift even stubborn deposits. Before you use it, rub the cut half of a lemon over the hob surface and leave for a few hours. The lemon juice will help loosen the remaining plastic and break down any grease on the surface. Once you've shifted it all using the scraper, clean the hob as normal. Finish by rubbing it down with the conditioning cloth (supplied with the scraper) to bring back the shine.

Q The special cleaner recommended for my ceramic hob is expensive. Can I use an everyday product instead?

A Definitely not. The toughened glass surface is extremely susceptible to scratching, and it's very, very important that you use a specialist hob cleaner such as Hob Brite, from supermarkets. These are less abrasive than general-purpose cleaners, so won't damage the glass, and also contain conditioners to polish the surface. For general cleaning, turn off the hob and make sure the surface is cool. (The only exception is with sugar-based spills when making jam or marmalade: turn off the heat immediately, remove the pan and, with extreme care, wipe the hob before continuing cooking. If you leave the sugar liquid, it will crystallize on cooling and pit the surface.)

It's important to clean the hob regularly to prevent dirt build-up. Kitchen paper or a clean damp cloth will remove light soiling, but never use a dishcloth wrung out in washing-up water – it'll contain sediment and grease that will smear and burn when the hob is turned on, making the surface look cloudy.

Really stubborn stains and cooked-on spillages should be tackled with a ceramic hob scraper. The Homecare Hob Brite Accessory Kit contains a scraper, conditioning cloth and spare blades. Don't use any other type of blade as it may not be sharp or flexible enough and could damage the glass.

Always lift and never drag pans when moving them around the hob and check the base is clean, dry and dirt-free. Although surface scratching won't affect the hob's performance, it'll spoil the look, and if cream cleaner gets trapped inside any of those tiny scratches, that will make the hob look cloudy and discoloured, no matter how hard you try to clean it.

Q How do I clean hard-water stains from my black Corian kitchen worktop?

A Use a damp cloth or sponge with a mild abrasive cleaner such as Bar Keepers Friend, from supermarkets. The secret ingredient is oxalic acid – found in rhubarb – which helps to break down the limescale and leave the surface smooth and shiny. Use a scouring pad only if you must – for really stubborn deposits – then rinse well and buff dry. Always restore the overall lustre afterwards: rub in a circular motion, using the cleaner to blend the scrubbed area into the surrounding surface.

Q The wooden draining board around my Belfast sink has black marks in the grooves. Is this mould? No matter how much I scrub I can't shift it – and I'm sure it's spreading. What can I do?

A Yes, it's mould caused by water penetration, probably because you haven't been oiling the wood enough. You need to scrub the grooves with very fine grade (0000) wire wool, dipped in lots of white spirit. Stubborn marks may need teasing out with fine sandpaper. Allow to dry (no need to rinse) and re-oil with a mixture of one-third boiled linseed oil mixed with two-thirds white spirit. Apply with a soft cloth and leave it to soak overnight, then remove any excess. Re-oil the wood every six months to stop it happening again.

Q How can I remove stains from a marble worktop? There are ring marks as well as greasy patches – it looks awful.

A At the risk of sounding like a press release from HG International, here goes: clean with a specialist marble cleaner, such as HG Marble Stain Colour Remover (around £7.29 for 500ml, 01206 795200; www.hg.eu for stockists). This will deal with discoloration from coffee, tea, fizzy drinks and red wine. For other stains, use HG Spot Stain Remover (around £5.82 for 500ml). Marble is very porous so, once it's clean, seal it with HG Top Protector (around £8.57 for 100ml). For day-to-day cleaning, never use washing-up liquid – it causes smearing and attracts dirt. Instead, use HG Marble Wash & Shine (around £7.33 for 1 litre).

Q **I spilt some superglue on my Formica kitchen work surface; when I wiped it off I made it worse and now I have a large stain. How can I get rid of it?**
A Simple: with something called Loctite Glue Remover, from DIY stores. It does exactly what it says on the tube and it's good for removing all types of glue. The people at Loctite assure me it can safely be used to remove the superglue from your work surface. Just squeeze a little on to the marked area, place a piece of kitchen towel over the top and leave overnight. The glue should dissolve and be absorbed into the paper towel. Rinse well with water afterwards.

Q **My two-year-old beech kitchen worktops are marred by dark rings caused, I think, by red wine. The wood was oiled by the installer and subsequently regularly by**

me, and has resisted other stains. How can I remove
them?

A Gently rub a little neat washing-up liquid into the stains
with a green scourer, rinse and leave to dry. You'll probably
have to re-oil the treated bits, but the worktops will look like
new. A little tip when re-oiling: lightly sand with fine sandpaper in the direction of the grain, then apply a thin film of
oil. (You can make your own: mix one part boiled linseed oil
from hardware shops with two parts white spirit – this will
keep for about six months, after which time it thickens too
much to soak in well.) This fluffs up the surface, and opens
the grain, allowing the oil to soak in and giving the worktops
a better chance against stains in the long run. Do this in the
evening so the oil can soak in overnight. Use only a thin film
– too little is way better than too much. In the morning,
remove any excess with a clean, dry, lint-free cloth.

Q We have oak kitchen worktops treated with Junkers
Rustic Oil. If any wet non-stainless-steel metal item is
left on the worktop it leaves a dark stain. How can I
remove it, short of sanding it out?

A Sounds as if you're not oiling your worktops often enough
and rust stains are penetrating the surface. Oak has an open
grain and needs frequent oiling. Sanding out the marks is really
the answer, although you can shift them with very fine grade
(0000) wire wool, dipped in white spirit, always going in the
direction of the grain. Treat an area slightly bigger than the

stain to try to blend it in (otherwise you'll end up with a light patch). Allow to dry (no need to rinse), then re-oil the surface either with your own oil or one part boiled linseed oil mixed with two parts white spirit. Apply with a soft cloth and allow to soak in overnight before removing any excess. Get into the habit of re-oiling every six to eight months.

Q My black granite kitchen surface is very difficult to keep clean – there are whitish marks I find impossible to remove. Even after I have 'cleaned' the surface, it always looks water-stained. What can I use that won't damage the granite but will remove marks and bring back the shine?

A These marks sound like 'ghost stains' – they disappear when wet but return when dry. The reason? Acid etching into the polished granite surface caused when you spill something acid-based, such as lemon or fruit juice, ketchup, vinegar or even via ring marks from the base of a cleaning bottle. If they're not too ingrained, try fine grade wire wool. Otherwise there's not much else you can do except have the surface reground, which is very expensive and not always possible.

Contact a stone specialist such as Extensive for advice (0845 2261488; www.extensive.co.uk), but before you take the leap, try Lithofin MN Power-Clean, £17.36 for 1 litre inc p&p from Extensive (as above), in case they are watermarks. Depending on how severe, use either neat or diluted (one part Power-Clean to 10 parts water). Apply and gently scrub with a green scourer, leave to react for a few minutes, then re-agitate. Rinse with lots of water, scrubbing as you go, then buff dry. But if the marks keep returning, you need to think about surface regrinding.

Q Our new home has a brown asterite kitchen sink/drainer that's seen better days. No matter how much we scrub away at it, the unsightly chalky-white residue won't shift. Any answers?

A It sounds like a build-up of limescale. The guys at Astracast, who made the sink (no longer in production), suggest you use neat clear vinegar or lemon juice. Apply with a cloth and leave for a few minutes before rinsing off. But don't expect instant results: you need to treat it every few days and be patient. Don't use a bought limescale remover as it could be too harsh for this type of surface.

Once clean, get into the habit of de-scaling the sink with lemon or vinegar each week, particularly if you live in a hard-water area. For everyday cleaning, use a non-abrasive, liquid cleaner and a soft cloth. No cream cleaners or scouring pads – they might scratch and mark the sink. For further advice, call Astracast on 01274 654700 or visit www.astracast.co.uk.

Q My Fragranite sink is badly stained. Nothing seems to work except Spontex pads, which are expensive and only partly shift the marks. Help!

A The guys at Franke, who make the sink, say staining is worse in hard-water areas, as limescale clings and, unless you deal with it, the sink gets stained with tea and coffee. Use a nylon brush with a proprietary limescale remover to shift the build-up. Don't use bleach as this only disguises rather than removes stains. Once the sink's looking good, clean regularly with Bar Keepers Friend, from supermarkets. Sprinkle around the damp sink, scrub to a paste with a nylon brush, then rinse thoroughly.

Q My Belfast sink is 10 years old and has become very difficult to clean. Stains will only shift if I leave a bleach solution in the sink overnight and then it looks grubby again the next day. It's driving me mad – what can I do?
A It sounds as if the glaze has worn away, exposing the porous stoneware underneath. One of the main culprits for this is the plastic washing-up bowl: it gathers grit on the bottom that grinds and scratches the sink's surface. Eventually, tea stains and suchlike get absorbed into the underlying material and make the sink much more difficult to clean, which is why you've had to resort to the bleaching every night (which has quite possibly further damaged the glaze). One alternative is a solution of biological washing detergent. Fill the sink with hot water, add a couple of tablespoons of powder, leave overnight, then rinse well. But, to be honest, I don't think you'll be happy until you've replaced the sink.

Q I have marks on my stainless-steel sink that look like water stains from the taps. Can you help?
A It sounds as if you have a build-up of hard-water deposits.

Stainless steel needs a bit of looking after, particularly if you have hard water. Pour some neat clear vinegar or lemon juice on to a paper towel, apply to the stains and leave for a few hours. Rinse thoroughly. Alternatively try bicarbonate of soda mixed with clear vinegar – brilliant on soap scum and water-marks. Aim for a toothpaste-like consistency (it froths and bubbles when first mixed). Smear on with a damp cloth or sponge, leave a few minutes, then rinse off and buff dry. It's also safe to use on glass, tiles and chrome. With either method, don't expect instant results: treat regularly and be patient.

Once it's clean, get into the habit of de-scaling the sink once a week, paying close attention to the area around the taps. Limescale can also be a problem if your taps drip, so replace any perished washers.

Q My stainless-steel kitchen sink has rust marks in the bowl and round the plughole, which I can't remove. I keep a washing-up bowl in the sink and probably don't clean it often enough. I thought stainless steel wasn't supposed to rust or stain. Any tips?
A Stainless steel does in fact stain – it just stains a bit less than other metals – and it can certainly rust. So although it's hard-wearing, it needs a bit of care. To remove the rust marks, try dabbing with clear vinegar or lighter fluid on a soft cloth. Rub gently, and rinse well.

To stop it recurring, make sure there's no debris in the sink after washing up, and always stand the washing-up bowl on end to allow the sink to dry out. And avoid using neat bleach, as it can attack the metal. If you must use it, dilute and rinse well afterwards.

Q **I scraped my brand-new ceramic butler's sink with an aluminium preserving pan as I was making marmalade. I've been left with silver scuff marks that won't come off with anything I've tried. Am I stuck with these marks for ever?**

A Not at all – all you need to do is, with the tap running, rub a wet pumice stone against the marks.

Q **Recently I bought two expensive, extremely sharp kitchen knives. I've not been able to maintain their keen edges and wonder how best to sharpen them?**

A Even the best knives dull with use and the initial factory edge lasts for only the first few weeks. Edge performance depends entirely on how it's sharpened. And sharp knives are safer; blunt blades need more force to cut, which increases the risk of the knife slipping and cutting you.

The best way is with a steel, but it takes practice to get the right angle. If you're right-handed, hold the steel horizontally in your left hand with the tip pointing slightly down. Holding the knife in your right hand, place the heel of the blade at the top of the steel at an angle of 20 to 30 degrees. Draw the knife down and across the steel, gradually pulling it away so that the tip ends at the tip of the steel. Repeat with the blade under the steel to sharpen the other side and alternate sides after every five or 10 turns until you get a razor-sharp edge. Keep the angle and run the full length of the cutting edge along the steel. Speed plays no part, so take your time. You may find it easier to use a sharpener that has slots to hold the blade at the correct angle. Here are a couple:

✳ Henckels Twinsharp Select Sharpener, around £30 (0845 2621731 for stockists): this uses a two-stage process. First, steel discs gently remove any minor damage and nicks, then ceramic discs polish the blade edge.

✳ Chantry Classic Knife Sharpener, around £27 (0114 2724221; www.premiercutlery.co.uk): a V-shaped slot with two spring-loaded steels that you run the blade between four or five times.

Q How can I clean the inside of a stainless-steel teapot that's become encrusted with tannin stains? It's too small for my hand to get in to scrub.

A Fill with hot (not boiling) water, add a tablespoon or a tablet of biological detergent and leave to soak overnight. Rinse well and, if necessary, use a nylon brush to shift stubborn deposits. For an extra sparkling finish, take a bottlebrush to the inside of the spout. Or fill with hot water, pop in a few denture cleaning tablets and soak overnight.

Q My terracotta teapot has stains at the spout. I'm reluctant to use bleach because I believe terracotta is porous. Help!

A It is, and you're right not to use bleach as it may affect the colour. Try soaking in a solution of De-Solv-It Crockery De-Stainer – call 01933 402822 for stockists. Just add 6 capfuls to a litre of fairly hot water and submerge the pot. Leave overnight for heavy stains. Rinse with hot water and then wash in warm soapy water before use.

Q What's the best way to clean the inside of a stainless-steel flask that's become badly stained with coffee?
A Never immerse a flask or put it in the dishwasher because

TOP TIP
How to clean the inside of a solid silver teapot...

Fill with a solution made with 4 teaspoons lemon juice to 100ml water; the acid will dissolve any water scale and get shot of the tea stains. Leave overnight, then scour and rinse.

If there's any tarnish (more likely if the teapot isn't used much) you'll need a proprietary silver cleaner such as Goddard's Silver Dip, from hardware stores. Pour into the teapot and swirl around for 10 seconds – no more. Rinse very thoroughly. (The dip can be reused, but for best results replace when it becomes discoloured.) A word of caution: don't use a silver dip on the inside of a silver plated teapot, as it can attack the lining.

water can get trapped inside the casing. Here are a few ideas to try instead. In each case, fill the flask with hot (not boiling) water and add one of the following before leaving it to soak overnight. Rinse well before you use.

✳ A tablespoon of Dri-Pak Borax Substitute (a natural cleaner and disinfectant), from hardware stores.

✳ A tablespoon of biological detergent or a dishwasher tablet.

✳ A few denture cleaning tablets.

One last tip: to stop stale smells forming, store with the stopper off so the air can circulate. If cleaning with washing-up liquid doesn't remove the smell of the last drink, fill the flask with warm water and add a few teaspoons of bicarbonate of soda. Leave to stand overnight, then wash in warm soapy water and rinse well.

Q Some of my Tupperware is stained from cooking with spices. How can I get it looking good again?

A Staining is tricky as the spice colouring gets absorbed into the plastic (the cheaper the plastic, the more difficult it is to remove). But here are a few things worth trying:

✳ Wipe with kitchen paper moistened with vegetable oil, then wash in hot soapy water.

✳ Wipe over with lemon juice (a natural bleaching agent). Leave a few minutes before washing off.

✳ Mix bicarbonate of soda into a paste by adding a little water and smear on the container. Leave on for an hour, then wash thoroughly in hot soapy water.

✳ Soak in a solution of Milton Sterilising Fluid. Add half a capful (15ml) for every 2.5 litres cold water and soak. Milton is non-toxic and won't leave a bad taste or smell.

Q How can I safely remove a stopper from a very expensive cut-glass decanter?

A First put on a pair of rubber gloves to protect your hands (they'll also help you grip). Wrap a very hot, damp cloth around the neck of the decanter to help expand the glass, then very slowly drizzle some vegetable oil around the stopper. Gently, gently wiggle and twist the stopper and I bet you it'll come free.

Q I have a cut-glass sugar sifter with a silver top, but can't get the top off in order to refill the base. My mother gave it to me in the 1950s and I have used it for many years. I can only assume that someone was a bit heavy-handed when replacing the top. How can I get it off and stop it becoming so fixed again?

A First put on a pair of rubber gloves – they'll protect your hands and help with grip. Wrap a very hot, damp cloth around the neck of the top to help the metal expand, and then firmly twist, and it should come free. To stop it sticking again, always make sure the screw threads are dry and free from sugar grains after refilling, and take care not to over-tighten the top or get it cross-threaded. Store in a cool, dry place.

Q Is there any hope for my late granny's brass jam-making pan? I badly burned the bottom making my last batch.
A It's easy. In your pan, bring to the boil a couple of table-spoons of biological washing powder mixed with a litre of water. Boil for 10 minutes, repeat if necessary, then rinse thoroughly, using a soft nylon brush to scrub off any deposits.

Brass can react with acidic foods such as fruit, which is why cookware is usually lined with tin or stainless steel. And if it's very old, it may even contain lead. So if yours is unlined, best keep it for display only.

Q How can I remove burnt strawberry jam from a non-stick preserving pan? I've managed to shift a little but there's still a circle about 4 inches in diameter that's proving very stubborn. I'm worried about damaging the non-stick coating.
A In your pan, bring to the boil a solution of biological washing powder or dishwasher detergent. Quantities aren't crucial, but let's say 1–2 tablespoons detergent, or a tablet, to about 2 pints of water. Boil for 10 minutes, repeat if necessary, then rinse thoroughly.

Q My non-stick frying pan is the worse for wear. How can I make it non-stick again?
A If it actually was a non-stick coating, there's nothing you can do – the process and cost involved mean it's far cheaper to replace. A non-stick coating is applied in layers and then has to

be cured at more than 40°C. And to get the coating to stick to the pan in the first place, the surface has to be roughened to provide a key; so worn-out pans can't just be put back on the production line. And although a worn non-stick surface loses its effectiveness, it's still safe: the coating is inert and won't harm you.

If, on the other hand, your pan is uncoated, you can restore its stick-resistance with the following method:

✳ Heat a handful of salt in the pan over a medium heat until hot.

✳ With a wad of kitchen towel, give the salt a good scrub around the pan (take care not to burn yourself). This will remove burnt-on deposits that can cause food to stick.

✳ Discard the salt and allow the pan to cool slightly before washing in hot soapy water. Rinse and dry.

✳ Heat again with enough oil to coat the surface. Once hot, carefully wipe out the excess with more kitchen towel.

✳ You're now ready to cook (add a little extra oil if you need to).

✳ Repeat as necessary.

Q **I have a copper pan I bought in Italy that's fabulous for making one-pot meals, but the lining is coming away from the inside. Where can I get it re-lined, and should I stop using it in the meantime?**

A Copper cookware is by far the best heat conductor and, yes, you should have it re-lined before using it again. Copper can react with acidic foods – when stewing fruit, for example – so cookware is usually lined with tin or stainless steel to act as a barrier (keep unlined pans for display only).

Divertimenti (020 7581 8065) offers a copper re-tinning service, which takes about three to four weeks (send your pan by registered mail). To work out the cost – charged at around £4.16 per inch for re-tinning or £6.80 per inch for re-tinning and polishing the exterior – measure the pan diagonally from the bottom of one side to the top of the opposite side (or across the top for frying pans). So if the measurement is 8in (20.5cm), the cost will be £33.28 or £54.40 including polishing.

Q I have a good-quality non-stick wok, but the last person who used it didn't oil the bottom and now it's rusty. Any hope?

A Plenty – rub the surface with the cut side of half a potato dipped in concentrated washing-up liquid. Rinse, then wipe with cooking oil and kitchen towel.

To keep your wok looking good, each time you use it wash in warm water without detergent. Dry thoroughly, then brush with a thin layer of oil. Store inside a plastic bag to stop dust sticking to the surface.

Q There's a nasty, sticky feel to our ageing oak-fronted kitchen cupboards. Up to now I've washed them with a sugar soap solution, which is okay for a short while but then the stickiness returns. Any advice?

A Golly, I wouldn't use sugar soap on oak – it's too abrasive and could wreck the finish. Instead, wash with a cloth rinsed in a warm solution of washing-up liquid with a little lemon juice or vinegar. Or a mild washing-soda solution. Don't let the wood get too wet, then rinse and buff dry. If you still have stickiness, use a hard wax polish and very fine grade (0000) wire wool. Test a hidden area first; if you're happy, use plenty of wax and gently rub in the direction of the grain. Remove the excess with a dry cloth and buff to shine. To keep the doors smooth, regularly wipe with soapy water (and rinse well).

Q I have a 1992 Magnet & Southern fitted kitchen, still in extremely good condition. However, the grained doors are not as white as they once were. Do you have a magic method to restore their whiteness?

A Painting them is probably your best bet. Use International One Coat Furniture & Cupboard Paint with Teflon, from DIY stores, as you don't have to sand down the surface beforehand or use a primer and, as it says on the tin, you only need one coat. Plus it's touch-dry in an hour. Just wash down the surfaces with warm soapy water, dry with a soft cloth and apply the paint using a natural bristle brush. It comes in eight colours, including white gloss/satin, and contains Teflon for extra resistance to knocks and scratches.

Q How hygienic are wooden chopping boards? Should I be cleaning mine in a particular way, or are plastic ones safer?

A Opinion is divided on which type is safer, but I believe it comes down to how well you clean it. You're fine with wood, as long as it's cleaned thoroughly and regularly after every use and wiped over occasionally with a sterilising solution, such as Milton, from supermarkets. (A plastic board can go in the dishwasher for a thorough clean, but otherwise treat in exactly the same way.) Germs can survive on boards for hours.

To clean your wooden board, scrub thoroughly after every use with very hot soapy water and rinse under very hot running water. (Never leave to soak: the wood will swell and crack on drying.) Dry with paper towels to avoid germs from a less-than-pristine tea towel. Leave to air, resting on its edge (it can warp if dried flat). To remove strong smells, squeeze lemon juice (or sprinkle mustard powder) on the board and wipe with a clean damp cloth. Always use separate boards for raw meat and veg, and replace a cracked, badly scored or stained board, whatever it's made from.

Q The brass rail along the edge of my kitchen worktop stays shiny for barely 24 hours after polishing. Can I use a sealant to make life easier?

A Brass fittings usually come with a lacquer finish to stop tarnishing. Protect the rail with a couple of coats of Rustin's Clear Metal Lacquer, from hardware stores, or call 020 8450 4666. Although not as durable as the lacquer applied in a factory, it will save on polishing. When it starts to break down after a year or so (usually unevenly), the rail will begin to tarnish again underneath. Strip the lacquer with paint remover, give the rail a clean with metal polish and apply new coats of lacquer. To keep the finished rails shiny, wipe over with a dish-cloth at the same time as you do the surfaces.

Q **My velvet-lined 50-year-old wooden cutlery canteen got damp and smells musty. It would be so nice to be able to use it again. The cutlery is Viners 'Silver Rose', c1957, in good condition. Can I have the canteen renovated?**
A If the interior is still good, you may be able to sort the smell with bicarbonate of soda: put 4–5 tablespoons in a shallow dish and place inside the empty canteen. Close the lid and leave for two to three weeks. If this doesn't work, contact Inkerman Silver of Sheffield (www.inkermansilver.co.uk; 0114 2720885), who offer a canteen-restoration service (the company also renovates cutlery). Prices vary depending on the work, but you can have the lining and fittings replaced and a copy of the original interior can be made if necessary. Allow up to four weeks.

Bathroom

Q My shower curtain is turning black – how can I clean it?
A Spray in situ with liquid washing soda crystals (from hardware stores and some supermarkets), leave half an hour, then rinse well.

For stubborn stains, machine-wash on a wool programme, adding a tablespoon of washing soda crystals (from supermarkets) along with the detergent. Bulk out the load with towels and add a cup of clear vinegar to the final rinse water to tackle limescale. Remove before the spin cycle and hang to let the creases drop out.

If the curtain is not machine washable, soak it in the bath for a couple of hours in a warm solution of soda crystals (2–3 tablespoons) with detergent. Rinse well. Or soak in a weak bleach solution (one part bleach to four parts water), making sure you rinse well to prevent damage from the bleach.

You should wash shower curtains down after every use and leave drawn until dry so the air can circulate. To keep fresh, machine-wash with biological detergent every month (or soak as above) to clean and stop mildew build-up.

Q My anti-slip shower mats (with suction caps) get really grubby, with orangey soap stains and mildew. I've tried bleach, coarse scrubbing and washing soda – all without success. How can I get them clean, and is it OK to put them in the washing machine?

A You need to face up to the fact that you're going to have to shell out for new ones. Mildew is hard to see off, but you could try scrubbing on both sides with hot soapy water and a nail brush. If heavily soiled, soak in the bath with a cup of biological washing powder (bleach could weaken the mat). Some mats are machine washable on a 40°C synthetic wash (check the instructions if you still have them). To stop it happening in future, always remove the mat after use and rinse it under the tap every single time to wash away soap deposits. Leave to dry, either hanging up or over the edge of the bath/shower rail so that the air can circulate freely – never dry near a radiator as it will crack the mat.

Q We've had our cast-iron bath resurfaced and were advised to get a bathmat without suckers. We can't find such a thing. Any ideas?

A Your adviser was right to tell you this as the bathmat suckers could cause the finish on the resurfaced bath to peel off. But a traditional bathmat has to have suckers, otherwise how else would it stick to the base of your bath? Luckily, there are alternatives.

You could have the bath's base treated with an anti-slip finish. It has to be professionally applied and preferably by the same company that did the resurfacing to ensure the solution doesn't react with the surface, but it can be done in situ. It involves spraying the base of the bath with an anti-slip solution which, once cured (after 24 hours), leaves a textured surface. Several companies carry out this service including Bath Renovation Ltd (020 7935 6590), which charges around £97 per bath but operates only in the M25 area; Bath Renovations and Management Services (02392 637058), with prices from £75 (it operates only in the South); Renubath Services Ltd (0800 1382202; www.renubath.co.uk), which charges around £45 (operates nationwide).

Alternatively, apply non-slip shapes. Renubath Services Ltd (details as before) can apply a series of anti-slip circles to the base of your bath. Available in creamy-white only, they cost around £30.

Q **I'm having difficulty finding a hair trap for my shower tray – any suggestions?**
A Lakeland sells one called the Dossil, £2.97 (01539 488100; www.lakeland.co.uk), suitable for the bath, shower or basin. Measuring 13cm across and made of silicone, it sits over the

plughole and stays in place until you want to remove it for cleaning.

Q We recently had an orbital shower cubicle installed. Due to all the other building work going on, we didn't clean the shower glass for a month. How can I remove the watermarks and keep the curved glass clean?
A Try bicarbonate of soda mixed with clear vinegar – brilliant on soap scum and watermarks. Aim for a toothpaste-like consistency (it froths and bubbles when first mixed). Smear on with a damp cloth or sponge, leave a few minutes, then rinse off and buff dry. It's safe to use on glass, tiles and chrome.

To keep your shower cubicle sparkling clean and free from watermarks, give the tiles and glass a quick swish over with a plastic-blade window wiper (from hardware stores) after every use. Alternatively, use the E-Cloth Shower Pack, from Home-base, John Lewis, Robert Dyas, Waitrose and Lakeland. It contains two microfibre cloths: one for cleaning, the other for buffing to a shine. No need for detergents, just use water. The cloths can be machine-washed (up to 90°C) and are also good on chrome, enamel and any shiny hard surface.

To make life even easier in the long run, treat the glass with Clear-Vision Shower & Boat Windows Kit, £24.42 inc p&p by mail order from Ritec (0845 2304888; www.clearshield.biz) – expensive and a bit of a faff, but it's a one-off treatment that stops limescale forming and should last up to two years. Apply after giving the shower a deep clean; it includes a protector that chemically bonds to the glass to repel water. This should mean you won't have to clean the glass so often, and when you do, it'll be less effort. The kit contains everything you need to treat two average shower cubicles.

Q We live in a hard-water area and have a water softener. Recently we had a power shower installed with a sliding glass door. The softened water leaves a spotty, milky deposit on the glass, resistant to limescale removers. Any ideas?

A It strikes me that your water softener isn't working properly – there shouldn't be the level of white marks and scale you get with hard water. ᵃ⁺ you do get should be easy to clean. Contact the softe | manufacturer for a testing kit (a test tube and a pack o| ually enough for about 10 tests). Fill the test tube w| ᵃter, drop in one of the tablets and give it a shake. I| turns green, it's soft and you have nothing to worŀ | ut if it turns red or murky brown, this shows you| ard and the unit could be faulty. Check the manual| an engineer if necessary.

Once you've done this| cleaning of the shower. Sponge down the door with equal parts clear vinegar and water. Leave a few minutes, then rinse and buff dry with paper towel.

Despite the water softener, you will get some light water marks and soap and grease residues, so to keep your shower sparkling, get into the habit of wiping down the door and tiles after every shower. A plastic window wiper is great for swishing the water off so that marks don't form.

Q The ceiling of my small shower room has mould spots. I've tried cleaning and even repainting, but after a few months, the mould reappears, despite running an extractor fan. Do you have any ideas?

A First you need to sort any structural damp, otherwise the mould will persist. Then treat with Polycell 3-in-1 Mould Killer, from DIY stores. This contains a fungicide to kill the spores and prevent regrowth. Wear safety glasses and protective gloves, and apply neat to the area with a brush, wetting the surface thoroughly (avoid drips). Wipe with a cloth or sponge to remove the mould (scrape with a blunt knife if it's tough), then allow to dry.

Next, apply Polycell Damp Seal. It's a one-coat, one-off treatment; apply with a brush over the stain and surrounding area. Allow to dry for five to six hours, then apply a paint designed for moist conditions, such as Dulux Bathroom +. For Polycell and Dulux stockists, call 0870 4441111 or visit www.polycell.co.uk or www.dulux.co.uk.

Q I have mildew in my shower. It is sealed with silicone and I have tried scrubbing with a toothbrush and even steam cleaning, but it won't shift. Any suggestions?

A The only thing I know that will remove those black stains is HG Mould Spray (call 01206 795200 or visit www.hg.eu for stockists), which also helps to control regrowth. Spray on the surface and leave it to work for several minutes. Repeat on badly affected areas after 20 minutes, then rinse off with plenty

TOP TIP

Is your bathroom a disaster zone? Do you suffer from mouldy grouting? Well, here's how to get rid of it...

Scrubbing grout lines with an old toothbrush dipped in a solution of half bleach, half water is good, but it won't stop the mould growing back, and you'll need to redo it every couple of months. For a more long-term solution, use a whitening product that contains a fungicide, such as Evo-Stik Grout Revive, from DIY stores. It comes in brilliant white, so will instantly freshen up grouting without the need for scrubbing, as well as keep mould at bay. Make sure the surfaces are clean, dry and dust free, and replace any old or loose grout before application. Apply an even coat of Grout Revive using the sponge tip, and allow three to four hours to dry before removing the excess with hot soapy water.

of clean water. Remove stubborn marks with a cloth or brush before rinsing.

Q My daughter had a lavatory installed by a cowboy builder. He has put something, perhaps grouting, in the bowl that has hardened into a solid lump. He refuses to return to fix this (and other problems). What can she do?

A I'm always amazed at the number of people who write to me about damage left by workmen. Fortunately you can sort this yourself, although what you use depends on what type of grouting it is. If it's cement-based you need HG Extra; for epoxy-based you need HG Spot Stain Remover (call 01206 795200 or visit www.hg.eu for stockists).

In both cases you need to empty the water from the toilet bowl first – bail out with an old yogurt pot or the like. Pour the cleaner in neat, enough to cover the deposit, and leave overnight. In the case of the HG Extra, this should dissolve the deposit so you can simply flush it away (this is okay to do as a one-off, but you shouldn't get in the habit of disposing large amounts of chemicals down the loo). If you use the HG Spot Stain Remover it will soften the deposit so you can use a plastic scraper to loosen it from the bottom. Wear rubber gloves and dispose of it in the bin.

Q **The inside surface of my lavatory bowl is scratched and has grey marks after a drain clearing company unblocked the loo. How can I remove these marks?**
A Fortunately you can easily sort this out: rub very, very fine sandpaper on the marks (and no, you won't be left with a new set of scratches).

Q **I've painted my horrid bathroom tiles with white satin tile paint. They now look great but I've dribbled paint on the bath and sink. How do I get it off without damaging the units?**

A You don't say whether the bath is acrylic or enamel, and I'm assuming the paint is oil-based. For the sink and an enamel bath, you can safely use white spirit or brush cleaner. Soak a pad of cotton wool with the white spirit and hold over the paint marks for a few minutes to soften the paint. Gently rub until removed, then immediately rinse with plenty of soapy water. However, don't use white spirit on an acrylic bath; it could dull the surface. Instead, take a plastic knife or plastic ice scraper (the sort for defrosting the freezer) and gently scrape away, taking extreme care not to scratch the surface. Don't use a metal scraper. Once the paint is gone, go over the area again with a cream cleaner to help polish out any light scratching.

Q We've had an interior opaque window installed in our bathroom but unfortunately handprints are evident, which I think are from the putty used when the glass was put into the frame. Can you suggest anything to remove the marks?

A Start by gently scrubbing the glass with a nylon brush (ideally a new one with stiff bristles) dipped in a warm solution of washing-up liquid. Use a circular motion and clean both sides if necessary. Rinse with clean water and buff dry. If this doesn't work, try using a mild acid such as clear vinegar or a mild solvent such as meths or white spirit. Apply with a soft cloth, taking care not to spill any on to the frame (if it accidentally runs down, quickly wipe it away). Finish by cleaning the window with a lint-free cloth and mild soapy water. Rinse and buff dry.

Q The person who laid the natural slate floor tiles in our bathroom didn't properly clean the grouting from the face of the tiles. Months have passed and it's now very stubborn to remove. Is there anything that will do it?

A You need Lithofin MN Builder's Clean from Extensive (0845 2261488; www.extensive.co.uk). It's an acid-based product that dissolves cement films and mortar residues from natural stone (but don't use it on limestone, travertine or marble). Dilute according to the instructions and sponge on to the surface (wear rubber gloves).

No need to scrub – just sit back and watch it fizz while it dissolves the cement residues (don't worry – it won't damage the tiles or existing grout!). Finish off by rinsing thoroughly with plenty of clean water, and you should have that beautiful slate floor back again.

Q My toddler has eczema, so I try to avoid using bleach and chemicals to clean the enamel bath he uses. Paraffin-based products leave a film on his bath toys. What should I do?

A Bicarbonate of soda is a good alternative for allergy-sufferers, and is fine to use on enamel (but test on a hidden area first). Sprinkle it around the damp bath, or mix with water to form a paste and apply with a damp cloth or sponge. Rinse well. You can soak the toys in a solution: fill the sink with hot water and add a tablespoon of bicarb (squirty toys should be regularly flushed through with a mild disinfectant to prevent mould). Otherwise use a proprietary eco-friendly cleaner such as Earth Friendly Products Cream Cleanser, £4.58 for 472ml inc p&p, from Allergy Matters (020 8339 0029; www.allergymatters.com). It's made from plant-based ingredients and contains lemon oil, which is great for cutting through dirt and grease, and is non-abrasive so it won't harm the bath.

Q I live in a hard-water area and the chrome taps in my beautiful new bathroom are being badly affected by limescale. How can I clean them?

A Mix equal parts clear vinegar and water and scrub on with a soft toothbrush. Rinse well and buff dry. For stubborn deposits, soak a cloth or piece of paper towel in the vinegar, wrap it around the tap, then cover with a plastic bag and secure with an elastic band. Fill the bag with vinegar if the inside of the tap is clogged too, making sure the limescale is in contact with the vinegar. Leave for an hour or so, then check on its progress, but don't leave overnight as it could damage the finish. Rinse thoroughly (use the toothbrush again if necessary) and dry. Alternatively, gently buff away deposits with a pumice stone. Don't worry; it won't scratch because the pumice is softer than the surface, but always test on a hidden area first.

These methods are safe to use on chrome-plated taps, but not on gold-plated taps or where the plate is wearing thin. Don't use on brass. Another word of caution: never use neat vinegar near enamelled surfaces because it can damage the finish. Always dilute the vinegar, check your progress and rinse often with water. Once clean, get in the habit of drying the basin, bath and taps with a towel after use to stop limescale building up again.

Q We've had a fancy glass handwash basin installed in the bathroom and it shows every single mark. How do I clean it without damaging the surface?

A It's fine to clean it with warm soapy water (ie washing-up liquid). But whatever you use, the glass will look messy every time you wash your hands. However, you can make life easier by keeping an E-Cloth at hand. It's a special microfibre cloth made from millions of tiny fibres that absorb dirt and grease, and has such a good natural cleaning effect that you need only use plain water. It's quick and easy – there's no rinsing and the highly absorbent fibres leave surfaces smear-free. So it's ideal for a quick once-over when you're rushing to get the place sorted for visitors. The cloth can be machine-washed (up to 90°C) and should last for years. There's a Bathroom Pack from Lakeland, John Lewis, Robert Dyas, Waitrose and B&Q, or online at www.e-cloth.com.

Start by cleaning the basin with the sponge cloth: just wring it out under the tap and use damp to remove soap scum, grease, watermarks and toothpaste. For a bit of extra sparkle, buff with the glass cloth which, incidentally, is also great for mirrors and stainless steel.

Q How do I clean the heads on my electric toothbrush? A disgusting black substance has formed deep inside the hollow part of the head. I leave them in a denture solution every night, but is there a better way?

A You could try soaking them in a mild solution of Milton Sterilising Fluid – dilute according to instructions and leave to soak overnight – but I would chuck them and start afresh.

After cleaning your teeth, rinse the brush thoroughly under running water with the handle switched on. Switch off and remove the head. Clean both parts separately by running water down the head shaft, behind the bristles and over the handle (the battery is sealed, so it's fine to rinse under the tap, just don't immerse in water). This will keep everything clean and stop toothpaste building up. Wipe dry before you reassemble the brush and put the handle back on the charger. You need to change the head at least once every three months, or sooner if the bristles splay. (Most have blue indicator bristles that fade with use and show you when to replace.)

Q I use hairspray in the shower room. I've noticed that when I clean the cistern and toilet seat lid, there's a rough residue, which I think is the result of spraying my hair. Nothing shifts it. Any ideas?

A Wiping over the surfaces with clear vinegar will do it. Apart from your shower room smelling like a chip shop for a while, everything will be back to normal.

Q Using vinegar, I removed brown stains from my white enamelled bath, but the glaze has come off, leaving a surface that's difficult to clean. How can I get the gloss back?

A Depending on how worn or damaged the bath is, you should be able to have it re-polished. This involves grinding away the dull top layer of enamel before sanding with a series of coarse and fine discs, ending with a lambswool mop to restore shine. It's not cheap (from around £175) and is suitable only for light-coloured, cast-iron baths in reasonable condition (badly damaged or worn baths, pressed steel or darker baths will need to be resurfaced, which costs from around £275). Companies that offer these services include: Bath Renovation Ltd (020 7935 6590), which operates around the M25; M&CT Ltd (01744 737274; www.vitreous-enamel.com) based in the Northwest but offers nationwide service; or Renubath Services Ltd (0800 1382202, www.renubath.co.uk); nationwide.

In future, if you get a limescale build-up, dilute one part vinegar to one part water, and even then, take great care. Use a soft cloth or soft toothbrush to rub the solution into the limescale a little at a time. Avoid getting the vinegar on the surrounding enamel surface and rinse the whole area often with clean water. It may take a couple of goes to shift every-thing. But the best cure is prevention: dry the bath and taps after each use to stop it forming in the first place.

For everyday cleaning, avoid products with anti-limescale ingredients, which may dull the enamel. Look for the 'V' logo of the Vitreous Enamel Association (01543 450596;

www.ive.org.uk) on cleaning products or visit its website for a list of cleaners that are safe for enamel baths.

Q My new acrylic bath has a slight scratch. It's barely visible until a bit of dirt gets in it, but then it really shows. What can I do to make it less noticeable?

A You should be able to smooth out the scratch with a cream metal polish or non-gel toothpaste. The mildly abrasive action will gently remove a thin layer from the top surface and help blend it in with the surrounding area.

Dab some on a soft duster and test a hidden area first (behind the taps is a good place), then if you're happy, gently rub over the scratch using a circular motion. Work in small sections at a time, wiping away the polish or paste often to check progress, and taking care not to rub too hard, or you could lose the sheen. Once you've finished, clean your bath in the usual way.

Q We've recently moved house and the newish plastic bath we've inherited has stains that will not shift. Help!

A Without seeing it and knowing what caused the stain, it's difficult to know how successful you'll be, especially if it's through to the fibreglass. However, you've nothing to lose, so here are some suggestions.

Try Bar Keepers Friend, from supermarkets. It's a wonderful powder cleaner for household stains (a little abrasive, so use with care); mix to a paste with water, leave for a few minutes, then rinse well.

Otherwise try a dab of cream metal polish, such as Brasso, from supermarkets, on a duster and rub very gently – the mild abrasion will help rub out the mark. Clean your bath in the usual way, rinsing well.

Still no luck? Call in Renubath Services Ltd (0800 1382202, www.renubath.co.uk), who operate nationwide.

Q My Jacuzzi bath is churning out horrible black gunk every time I use it. Help!

A Deposits such as hair and oils (won't go into any more detail!) build up in the pipework, hence the gunk. First check with the manufacturer whether they recommend a particular cleaner. If not, try Whirlpool Maxus from Giardino (01952 820061; www.giardino.co.uk). Run the bath, add the fluid and leave overnight. Do this twice a year. Giardino also makes Whirlpool Clear, which leaves a thin film inside the pipes to help reduce this build-up – use every four to six weeks.

The other problem is the growth of potentially harmful bacteria inside the pipes – ideally you should sterilise after every bath, but at least once a week. Either use a product such as Whirlpool Crystal, again from Giardino, or fill the bath and add a cupful of mild sterilising liquid such as Milton (it won't harm the metal). Switch on the jets for five minutes, then empty the bath, refill with clean water and circulate for a further five minutes to rinse.

Q My enamel bath had a stain, so I put some toilet cleaner on it overnight (don't ask me why – worst decision I ever made). It's now very white, but the enamel has been stripped away and the surface is pitted. Any ideas?

A It's possible to sort this, but not cheap. You have options, depending on whether your bath is made of steel (chances are it is) or cast iron (rare nowadays).

✳ Depending on how extensive the damage is, you may be able to have the bath re-polished. This is done in situ and involves grinding away the top layer of enamel before sanding the surface with a series of coarse and fine discs, ending with a lambswool mop to help restore shine. The cost is around £175, and it's suitable only for white cast-iron baths. Contact the Institute of Vitreous Enamellers (01543 450596; www.ive.org.uk) for approved companies.

✳ Have the bath resurfaced. Although less expensive than re-enamelling (see below), the finish isn't as hardwearing, though it should last between five and 11 years. Again, the process is done in your home and takes about five hours, and you won't be able to use the bath for 24 hours. It involves cleaning and grinding the existing enamel, spraying with several base coats and finishing with a special acrylic or epoxy resin. Several companies offer this, including Renu-bath Services Ltd (0800 1382202, www.renubath.co.uk), who provide a nationwide service. It costs around £400.

✳ Have the bath re-enamelled. This is the most expensive and disruptive option (you have to send the bath to a factory to be kiln-fired, which costs around £650 plus transport). It's unsuitable for steel baths (and cheaper to buy a new one), but if it's a special cast-iron bath it'll be as good as new with a very durable finish. The process involves shot-blasting to remove the existing enamel, before the bath is re-coated with a minimum of three layers of new vitreous enamel. Each layer is fused to the surface by heating to above 750°C. Contact the Institute of Vitreous Enamellers (as above) for a list of approved companies.

In future, only use cleaners with the 'V' logo of the Vitreous Enamel Association on the label, or visit www.ive.org.uk for a list of cleaners safe for enamel baths.

Laundry

Q My eau-de-nil damask tablecloth has a red wine stain which I tried to remove with a standard stain remover but all it did was turn the stain blue. How can I get the mark out?

A You may have actually set the stain in your gallant attempts to remove it, but have a go with Wine Away from Lakeland (01539 488100; www.lakeland.co.uk). The mark will at first stay blue but then eventually fade. All you do is spray on, leave for a few minutes, then wash as normal. You might have to repeat this a few times.

Next time you have a red wine spill, flush it out straight away with sparkling water. And never sprinkle with salt – it could permanently set the stain. Just make sure you always have a bottle of sparkling water in the house and throw it over, followed by a treatment of Wine Away.

Q I attended a wedding a few weeks ago where the florist hadn't removed the stamens from the lilies. A bridesmaid laid her bouquet on a chair that my boyfriend later sat on and his new machine-washable, linen-mix suit is ruined. The seat of the trousers is covered in pollen, which I tried to remove with sticky tape, but, in places, it must have come into contact with water, so the stains are set in. Help!

A You did all the right things – gently patting the pollen with sticky tape and avoiding the temptation to rub with a damp cloth – but, as you've discovered, once it gets wet, it's hard to shift. However, as the suit is machine washable, there are a couple of stain removers that might work. Try Dylon All-purpose Pre-wash Stain Remover, or Dr. Beckmann Stain Devils for Mud, Grass & Make-up, both available from supermarkets. Incidentally, simply washing on a 40°C cotton cycle (after using sticky tape) will work on light stains, but since the pollen is set in, you should pre-treat the stains before washing. When you do wash the trousers, throw in the jacket at the same time – if any dye should be lost during the cycle, this will reduce the risk of the pieces fading by different amounts.

Q My son plays a lot of football and comes home with mud and grass stains on his white kit, which is hell to remove. Can you suggest anything?

A The first rule is to act sharpish! Soak the kit overnight in cold water – often the stains will come out by doing that, then washing at 40°C with a biological detergent, although it wouldn't do any harm to add a couple of scoops of OxiClean Versatile Stain Remover, around £3.49 a 500g tub from supermarkets. If the stains are really ground in, then soak the kit in OxiClean for up to six hours before washing it (this should work on the grass stains too). If the mud is caked on, let it dry first, then brush off what you can before soaking. A little tip: for grass stains on white leather trainers or tennis shoes, spray the mark with a few drops of WD-40 and wipe with a clean cloth.

Q A favourite cotton skirt got caught in my bicycle chain and now has black grease marks. I've soaked it in stain remover twice, which has helped, but there are some marks that just won't go. Any ideas?

A As you've discovered, bicycle grease is stubborn, and you'll need a strong stain remover. Try either Dr. Beckmann Stain Devils for Grease, Lubricant & Paint, from supermarkets or online at www.dr-beckmann.co.uk, or White Wizard from Lakeland (01539 488100, www.lakeland.co.uk). After treatment, wash your skirt as normal using a biological detergent (you might need to repeat a few times).

Q I'm a 36-year-old male who sweats a lot! I use an antiperspirant but my shirts have become stiff and yellow under the arms. I've tried various remedies, but all in vain. Any suggestions?

A Not surprisingly, it's a combination of your sweat and the deodorant – solid sticks are the worst offenders. Things get

TOP TIP

How to keep your towels soft and fluffy...

The lack of fluffiness is caused by hard water (the harder the water, the harder the towels) and soap residues that build up over time. First soak the towels in the bath in a solution of water softener, such as Calgon, from supermarkets, then rinse thoroughly. Now wash as normal using the maximum recommended amount of detergent. Don't use conditioner: far from softening the towels, it builds up and reduces absorbency.

To keep up the fluff factor, check you're using enough detergent, and each time add half a cup of clear vinegar to the first rinse (don't put it in the conditioner compartment as this is released in the final rinse). You'll have to keep an eye on your machine to get the timing right, but a good guide is to tip it into the detergent drawer while the machine is filling with water. This is done commercially, which is probably why hotel towels always seem so lovely and fluffy.

Finally, rinse and spin the towels well – the higher the spin, the softer the towels will be, as you're spinning more of the hard water impurities out. Then tumble-dry – this gives the softest towel as it opens up the terry loops. Dry on a medium heat, then finish on high for the last few minutes. Failing that, line-dry to fluff up the fibres, but never put towels on the radiator, as they'll get hard.

worse if you put your deodorant on *after* you get dressed or don't wait for it to dry before dressing.

Soak colourfast items overnight in Bio-tex Stain Removing Powder, from supermarkets – it helps break down the protein in the sweat and loosens the deodorant. Gently scrub the area with a nailbrush, then wash with biological detergent. If this doesn't work, try adding Vanish Oxi Action Intelligence (again, from supermarkets) to the wash along with detergent. For really stubborn stains, work in some of the stain remover or use a solution of one part glycerine to one part warm water and leave for an hour before washing.

Q There's a chicken curry stain on my pale blue woollen jumper, which I've tried treating with stain-removing products. Although the mark has faded it's still clearly visible. Any ideas?

A Curry is a toughie to remove. And with wool you're restricted to the gentler, shorter wash programmes that'll struggle even with the most efficient stain remover. But it's worth having a go at sponging the stain with meths to dissolve as much colour as possible (curry stains are usually caused by the pigment curcumin, found in turmeric). The mark will turn bright red initially; this is normal. Flush with cold water, then apply a mild detergent solution to the stained area. Allow to soak in for a few minutes, then machine-wash at as high a temperature as the jumper will allow. If it's still not completely gone, curcumin is unstable under light, so put the jumper in direct sunlight for a few days and, with luck, it'll fade further.

Q All my silk ties have some sort of food or wine stain. Is there a home remedy?

A If they're not hideously expensive, you might get away with gentle handwashing in biological detergent (though they may lose a bit of body). Don't rub or wring otherwise you could damage the fabric or misshape the linings. Soak in a solution of 2 teaspoons of clear vinegar to 3 litres of water after the final rinse to preserve the colour. Leave for a few minutes, then roll up in a clean, dry towel. Use a warm, dry iron while still damp (steam might leave marks).

Alternatively, try Silk & Clean, from Tie Rack or Marks & Spencer. A quick wipe with the disposable pad should remove most marks. As with all stain removers, test on a hidden area first.

Q I spilt olive oil on my green silk jacket – how can I get rid of the stain?

A First pre-treat it, particularly if you use a handwash or silk programme on your machine as the shorter, gentler wash won't remove the stain on its own.

Use Dr. Beckmann Stain Devils Cooking Oil & Fat from supermarkets or online at www.dr-beckmann.co.uk, then wash the jacket as normal using a biological detergent. (You should not generally use bio detergents on silk. They have enzymes that break down protein – blood, egg, milk and so on – and oil, but which also weaken protein fibres such as silk, wool and cashmere.) As with all stain removers, test on a discreet area first.

Q My wife cooks with lots of olive oil. How does one remove stains from clothing that remain after several washes?

A I doubt you'll succeed with the clothes that have been washed several times. In future, pre-treat with a stain remover before washing. Try White Wizard, from Lakeland (01539 488100, www.lakeland.co.uk) or Dr. Beckmann Stain Devils Cooking Oil & Fat, from supermarkets or online at www.dr-beckmann.co.uk. Test for colour fastness first.

Q While I was carving the Sunday roast, some fat dripped on to my suede shoes and left a stain. How do I get it out?

A You need Woly Suede Cleaner (01858 467467; www.shoe-stringuk.com). It's an intensive foam shampoo containing a degreaser to remove fat, oil and tar spots. Spray on to a cloth and rub over the whole surface of both shoes (to avoid patches), paying particular attention to the stained area. Allow to dry – don't rinse off – then use a suede brush to restore the nap.

If your shoes were pre-treated with a stain protector, you'll probably get away with just the suede cleaner. If not, and the stain's still there, try using Woly Gum Suede Block (stockists as above). This is like a pumice stone and is designed to remove watermarks and grease. Give a good rub over the mark; don't worry about shedding – this is just the block wearing down and not bits of suede. Tidy up with a suede brush before cleaning with the suede cleaner again. Finally, spray with a protector to repel water and help guard against future Sunday lunch spillages.

Q I have a glue mark on my new top – it's either Pritt Stick or clear school glue. I tried ironing it through a hankie, but that only made it worse. The top is 95 per cent viscose and 5 per cent elastane. Any suggestions?

A Pritt Stick and other water-soluble adhesives should come out with water. Once dry, soak in cool water for a day or two to soften the glue before washing as normal.

Ironing probably wasn't the best idea, but you may still be in with a chance. Copydex is waterproof, though, so for this you'll need a solvent such as Mykal Sticky Stuff Remover from John Lewis (08456 049049) to break it down before washing.

Q How can I remove chewing gum from my wool sweater? I picked off the worst bits before washing it, but there's still more to come.

A Put the sweater in the freezer and, when the gum is brittle, pick it off. Didn't work? Gently scrape off with a blunt knife. Still some there? Use Dr. Beckmann Stain Slayer from supermarkets or online at www.dr-beckmann.co.uk. Spray on, rub until evenly dispersed and then rinse thoroughly with warm running water. Wash as normal.

Q My washing line is under a tree, and unfortunately birds like to use the clothes as target practice. How do I get the mess off my son's school shirts?

A Bird poo can be a sod to shift, but as long as the shirts are white or colourfast and not nylon, try immersing in a solution of hydrogen peroxide, available from chemists (one part 20-vol peroxide to six parts cold water) for no longer than 30 minutes. Wash and rinse thoroughly.

Q Any tips on how to remove build-up, caused by stick deodorant, from my bras? It seems to form a layer on the edge where the bra fits under the armpit.

A Try using White Wizard from Lakeland (01539 488100, www.lakeland.co.uk). With a nail brush, very gently work some of the cream into the stained area, then wash as normal with your usual detergent.

Q I put my white denim jacket in the washing machine with a lipstick in the breast pocket. Now I have a pink stain. I've rewashed it at 60°C but no luck. Any ideas?

A Try washing it again, but this time pre-treat the stain with something like De-Solv-It Universal Stain Remover & Pre-wash. Not sure how successful you'll be as you may have set the stain by washing it at 60°C, but you have nothing to lose.

Q I'm going crazy with yellow sunscreen stains appearing on white cotton and linen clothes after washing. I've tried cooler washes and pre-rinsing but have still managed to ruin a new white linen shirt. Can you help?

A It's not the cream itself that causes the staining, it's the water you use for washing. The water's metal ions react with the active ingredients in the suntan cream and turn it yellow (which is why the stains appear *after* washing). Water types and creams vary, so staining may not always be a problem; you might have this at home but not on holiday.

Regular washing will eventually fade the marks, but to stop it happening again, pre-treat areas you think may have come into contact with suntan cream (around arms and neck, for example) with Dr. Beckmann Stain Devils Cooking Oil & Fat from supermarkets or online at www.dr-beckmann.co.uk. Wash as normal.

Q I have a pair of khaki trousers that sport a conspicuous blob of blue ballpoint ink. I've heard that alcohol will remove it, but I'm worried it will affect the colour of the fabric. What could I use instead?

A Ballpoint ink can be very difficult to get rid of: you must, must, must act quickly and even then you're not guaranteed success. In my experience the proprietary stain removers, including those specifically designed to remove ballpoint pen, don't work well on cotton. However, as you don't have much to lose, one of my home remedies might just rescue your trousers.

✳ Dab with a damp cloth moistened with milk, then wash as normal.

✳ Dab lightly with a cotton wool bud moistened with meths, avoiding spreading the stain; wash as normal.

✳ Try gently dabbing with some cotton wool moistened with a solution of hydrogen peroxide, available from chemists (one part 20-vol peroxide to six parts cold water), but don't use on nylon and soak for no longer than 30 minutes. Machine wash as normal.

✳ Rub the area with lemon juice and rinse thoroughly. Keep repeating until clear.

✳ Machine washing should eventually fade the mark. If possible use a high temperature and a biological detergent.

✳ Have the trousers dry cleaned.

✳ If all else fails, contact the manufacturer of your pen for advice.

Q **I used a thick woollen wrap from Egypt (a tight weave – almost like a mat) as a table runner at a dinner party. As the night (and drinking) progressed, candle wax spilled on to it. I tried scraping it off, but it's gone right through the fabric. Any thoughts?**

A Your best bet is to re-melt the wax and tease it out with a warm iron. Make sure you've scraped away all the surface gunk first, using a blunt knife, then place a few sheets of kitchen paper on either side of the stain. With a hottish dry iron, gently press over the area, moving the paper around until all the wax has been absorbed. Take care not to let the iron touch the fabric. Remove any remaining colour with a dab of meths, but test on a hidden area first. Then treat your wrap to a dry clean.

Q My husband wears hair wax, which has given our Egyptian cotton pillowcases a nasty yellow tinge. How can I get them back to pristine white?

A Most waxes are oil-based, so washing with a liquid biological detergent should do it – use a little of the liquid to pre-treat the fabric before putting in the machine. Do a cool wash first and if that doesn't work try a hotter wash (not the other way round as the hot wash could set the stain).

If this doesn't do it, treat the pillowcases with a stain remover either before or during the wash, such as Vanish ActionBall Tablets – add one with your usual detergent; OxiClean Versatile Stain Remover – add a scoop, ditto; or De-Solv-It Universal Stain Remover & Pre-wash – spray on both sides of the cases and leave for a few minutes before washing as normal. All these products are available from most supermarkets.

Q I used fake tan recently and must have spilt it on my woollen bed throw. Can you help?

A The active ingredient in fake tan develops on fabric in the same way as it does on your skin. Don't dry-clean the throw as the solvents could react with the fake tan and worsen things. Instead, handwash in warm water using biological detergent (in the bath if the throw is very big) – that will help remove the grease and oils from the fake tan. Treat any remaining marks with a proprietary stain remover such as Dylon Stain Remover for dry-clean fabrics, from supermarkets, and wash again. Test on a hidden area first.

Q The dye from my coloured handbag has transferred to my clothes and is difficult to remove. What can I do?
A Without knowing what type of leather it is, it's difficult to say whether this is happening because the bag is faulty, since nubuck, suede and unfinished leathers naturally leach colour. I would take the bag to the shop to ask for my money back, plus a refund of any bills for dry cleaning the stained clothing. Your local Trading Standards department may be able to support you.

To stop it continuing, you need to seal the colour with something like LTT Satin Gloss (don't worry – it won't give too high a gloss) or Matt Finish from LTT Leather Care (01423 881027; www.lttleathercare.co.uk). These are one-off treatments, but are unsuitable for suede or nubuck. Test a hidden area first (say underneath) as it could change the colour. If you're happy, spray evenly over the surface and allow to dry thoroughly. To keep the bag in great condition, use LTT Handbag Cleaning Kit (stockist as above), which includes a cleaner and protector. Again, this is no good for suede or nubuck.

Now to the dye on your clothes. If they're washable, try a colour run remover, such as Dr. Beckmann Colour Run Remover from supermarkets or online at www.dr-beckmann.co.uk, but I can't guarantee success. Use either in the machine or leave to soak for up to an hour, then wash as normal.

Q My daughter brought back leather belts from Morocco, but they leave marks on clothes. What can we do to stop this?

A You need to seal the colour with something like LTT Satin Gloss (gives a shine without too much of a gloss) or Matt Finish from LTT Leather Care (01423 881027; www.lttleathercare. co.uk). It's a one-off treatment but, without knowing what type of leather has been used, it could change the colour, so test on a small area. If it's a thumbs-up, spray evenly over the whole surface and leave to dry.

If dye is still in the clothes, try a colour run remover such as Dr. Beckmann Colour Run Remover for coloureds, from supermarkets or online at www.dr-beckmann.co.uk. Either use the colour run remover directly in the machine or leave to soak for an hour, then wash as normal.

Q The house got damp this summer, leaving mildew spots on my seldom-worn leather gloves. How do I get rid of them, and how should I store them in future?

A Gently rub off surface mould with a soft cloth – outdoors so you don't inhale spores. If it has penetrated and stained the leather, hold each glove over a boiling kettle (wear oven gloves for protection) and allow the steam to penetrate the leather – the heat will kill the spores and stop them spreading.

Next, wash the gloves (most are made of washable leather, but check instructions) to remove any staining. Prepare a luke-warm solution of soapflakes, put on the gloves, immerse your hands in the solution, rub gently together to remove dirt, then rinse well. Take the gloves off and press them between towels to remove excess moisture. Allow to dry naturally at room temperature (not on a radiator). As they are drying, gently stretch them until almost dry, then put them on your hands to restore the shape. (This can be done with both leather and suede gloves.)

Regarding future storage, you'll need to deal with the damp or you'll be back where you started, but otherwise just lay them flat in a drawer. You can wrap them in acid-free tissue paper (£10 for 25 sheets from Total Wardrobe Care, 0207 4984360; www.totalwardrobecare.co.uk), but it's not essential.

Q **I like to wear leather-palmed gloves for driving. In the past I have bought small plastic bottles containing a liquid that cleaned them efficiently when soaked in water. I can't find it in the shops any more – what can I use instead?**

A You can wash your leather gloves in a lukewarm solution of soapflakes (such as Dri-Pak Soap Flakes or Dri-Pak Pure Liquid Soap, from supermarkets and hardware stores).

Put on your gloves, immerse in the solution and rub your hands gently together to remove dirt, then rinse well. Take them off and press between towels to remove excess moisture.

Allow to dry naturally at room temperature (never on a radiator as that will make the leather hard). As the gloves are drying, gently stretch them until almost dry, then pop back on to your hands to restore the shape. This method can be used for both leather and suede gloves, and the secret is to wash them before they get too dirty.

Q **I washed my favourite cardi in too-hot water and now it has felted. Anything I can do?**

A Once felted there's not much hope – the fibres have been damaged. But if it's not too bad, you may be able to tease the cardigan back to respectable proportions. One approach is to try washing it again, using loads of fabric conditioner in the rinse water to try to relax and stretch the fibres. Blot with a towel, pull back hard into shape, and dry flat away from direct heat and sunlight. Or you could soak it in a solution of Dri-Pak Borax Substitute, from hardware stores, which will soften the water. To make the solution, dissolve a quarter of a cupful of the borax in a bowl of warm water and soak the cardi for at least half an hour. Rinse in cool water, blot with a towel and dry as above.

Q **I was advised to wash my new angora sweater in cold water before wearing to prevent it shedding. I did, but the fibres still strayed everywhere. How can I avoid this?**

A Angora wool comes from the soft fur from the angora rabbit (angora goats produce mohair), and is thought to be three times warmer than lambswool. However, as you've found, there's a price to pay. The yarn is spun with a low, soft twist, which means fibres can break off more easily during wear.

The good news is that with time and careful handwashing the shedding will subside – honestly! Avoid dry cleaning as this strips oils from the wool, and exacerbates things. Wash in lukewarm water, using a wool detergent, rinse well, then roll in a clean towel to remove excess moisture. Dry flat, away from direct heat and sunlight.

Q My white cotton sheets are looking distinctly non-white, particularly against newly bought pillowcases. The labels say not to bleach, so how can I get them white again?
A There are a few reasons for this loss of brightness. First, you may not be using enough detergent. If so, this will cause dirt removed during the wash to be re-deposited on to the sheets. Or, if you live in a hard-water area, calcium deposits may have built up and caused greyness. To restore whiteness, re-wash using the maximum dose at the highest recommended temperature, soaking the load first in a softener such as Calgon.

Still grey? Try using Dr. Beckmann Glowhite, five sachets from supermarkets or online at www.dr-beckmann.co.uk. The non-bleach formula claims to restore whites even at low temperatures. You put a sachet in with your wash, then add detergent. To keep them bright, follow the recommended detergent dose for your water hardness and don't overload the machine. If you have very hard water, it's a good idea to carry out an idle wash periodically, with detergent but no clothes, to help reduce scale build-up.

Greyness can also be caused by dye transferring from a non-fast colour. Even at low temperatures, small amounts can bleed on to other items and, although it may not be noticeable in one wash, whites soon begin to look grey and dingy. Re-wash at the hottest recommended temperature and, as always, separate from coloureds. If your sheets have coloured detail, put a Colour Catcher sheet (from major supermarkets) in the wash along with your usual detergent to attract any loose dye.

Oils and grease from hair and body can also build up on laundry if you don't use enough detergent or the right sort, wash at too low a temperature or overload the machine. Re-wash in smaller loads using the maximum dose of a biological detergent and the hottest temperature possible, according to the label. For an extra boost, pre-treat problem areas with a liquid biological detergent or proprietary stain remover. Alternatively, add half a cup of Dri-Pak Borax Substitute (from hardware stores) to your wash. It acts as a water conditioner and has a natural mild brightening and whitening effect.

Q I want to lend my son's christening robe and shawl to my sister, who's about to give birth. However, both items have yellowed in places, even though they were kept in a plastic bag in a closed cupboard away from sunlight. The robe is 100 per cent polyester and the shawl 100 per cent acrylic. How can I get them back to their original white?

A I hate to say it, but the discoloration is probably permanent. You could try handwashing the items with biological detergent and a stain booster such as Vanish Oxi Action Intelligence, from supermarkets, or have them dry cleaned, but I'm not optimistic.

Keeping them out of direct sunlight was a good idea, but if you want to store precious garments over a long period, they need to be wrapped in acid-free tissue paper and placed in a pH-neutral box. These are available by mail order from The Empty Box Company (01306 875430; www.emptybox.co.uk), £30.90 for their Christening Robe Box (plus p&p). Keep in a cool cupboard – but not in the loft because of temperature changes – and away from direct or indirect sunlight and damp. Check on them every 18 months, refolding along slightly different lines to help stop permanent creasing.

Q How can I reverse the yellowing of cotton by sunlight? Bleach isn't working.
A This happens if white cotton is exposed to direct sunlight for a long time. The yellowing is caused by the UV from the sunlight degrading the brightener on the fabric and turning it yellow. This can happen with new items, since they have brightener added to make them look ultra-white, or with older items that have been washed in detergent containing brightener (most do, except those for coloureds). To reverse yellowing, try rewashing in detergent containing optical brighteners or brightening agents (may take more than one

go). Wash within a full load, using the recommended dose, and at the hottest temperature on the label. But remember to keep away from direct sunlight if line-drying, and take inside as soon as it's dry.

Q On a recent holiday in China, I bought a beautiful silk-filled duvet – with no care instructions. Can I wash it?
A Unless it gets very dirty, you shouldn't have to clean it. Instead, air it outside on a good day for 20–40 minutes a few times a year (the same for feather-filled duvets). This will keep the filling fluffy and, to an extent, counter the moisture and odours we give off during sleep. Avoid strong sunlight as this can over-dry the filling.

If the duvet has a non-removable patterned cover, use as a quilt with a top and bottom sheet. Mop up any spills immediately to avoid them soaking through the filling. If the casing does get stained, spot-clean using a mild, non-biological detergent for delicates: add a small amount of detergent to a warm basin of water, immerse only the stained section, and gently squeeze until clean. Rinse thoroughly, then sandwich between a couple of towels to absorb excess moisture (don't wring). Dry flat, but keep gently moving the filling with your fingers to stop it from matting (use a warm hairdryer). Never vigorously shake a silk-filled duvet as it could tear the fleece filling.

Don't wash it either at home or in a launderette as it will become extremely heavy and could tear. If overall cleaning is necessary, dry clean only as a last resort. Once you get it home, air for at least a couple of hours to get rid of any solvent odours before putting it back on the bed.

Q My new polyester-lined outfit clings to my body. What can I do to stop this?
A Static build-up is caused by the combination of positive and negative ions in your clothes, and silk and synthetic fibres are big culprits. If the outfit is machine-washable, add fabric conditioner to the final rinse, and avoid over-drying: remove items from the dryer while still damp, and air-dry or use anti-static tumble-dryer sheets. Moisturising your skin will help, as will wearing a cotton slip. If the static has already built up, brush with a wire coat hanger. Alternatively, John Lewis sells GO-Stat Anti-Static Spray, which can be used on all fabrics and lasts for at least 24 hours.

Q My washing machine isn't taking all the detergent from the drawer each time it's used. I live in a hard-water area, use water softener and wash the drawer out about once a month. Anything else I should be doing?
A If you use tablets, check the box to make sure you're using them correctly. Not all types go in the drawer; some have to go inside a net bag and be placed on top of the washload. And check you're storing them in a dry place: detergent goes sticky and sets hard if allowed to get damp. If none of these is the problem, the water jets inside the dispenser drawer may be blocked with limescale. This reduces the water flow, meaning

there's not enough to flush the detergent into the drum. Using a water softener such as Calgon will help protect the heating element and other vital machine parts, but it won't stop limescale building up on the jets. The problem's worsened if your machine is hot and cold fill, as the jets will scale up more quickly than if you have cold feed only.

To clean, mix a solution of equal parts clear vinegar and water. Remove the drawer and scrub the solution on to the roof of the dispenser compartment using a nylon brush. Then run an idle wash (empty drum, hottest programme and maximum dose of biological detergent) to help flush things through. Repeat, every month or so, when you clean out the drawer.

Still clogging? Maybe your water pressure has been reduced, say if plumbing work has been done in the house; otherwise check with your local water authority.

Q Could you tell me why, with every steam iron I buy, I get splashes of brown water even though I empty the iron after each session? And why do those splashes always seem to affect my white ironing?
A Firstly, accept a gold star for bailing out after each session, but this actually isn't enough on its own. The iron acts like a vacuum, sucking up fibres and impurities from your clothes as you work and, over time, these then build up and discolour the water inside the tank – hence the brown splashes that seem to appear only when you're doing the whites. You need to get into the habit of using the self-clean function on your iron –

say at every second session. This forces water and steam through the holes in the soleplate and flushes out any deposits. Most irons over £25 have this feature, and if yours doesn't, it's worth buying one that does.

Use ordinary tap water – you need an element of hardness in the water to get a good jet of steam – and avoid using scented, softened, pure distilled or demineralised water or rainwater. These contain organic waste or mineral elements that can cause spitting, brown staining, or premature wear to your iron. If you live in an area with very hard water, mix tap water with shop-bought distilled water or demineralised water in equal parts, which will reduce scale build-up.

Q I've wrecked my steam iron with rubber residue from a T-shirt motif. It now has a gloopy black mess over the holes. I've tried lots of things, but it won't budge. The iron still works, but it smells when warm. Can you help?
A Heat the iron on a warm setting and rub it across a damp, loosely woven cloth or coarse towel held taut over the edge of your ironing board. If necessary, gently rub the soleplate with a damp plastic scourer, but take care if it has a non-stick coating.

Otherwise, use a proprietary soleplate cleaner such as Hot Iron Cleaner from Lakeland (01539 488100; www.lakeland.co.uk). Most are suitable for all soleplates, but if yours is non-stick, check the label. Work in a well-ventilated room – some of the cleaners give off fumes.

Q I managed to scorch my new pure cotton white shirt while ironing it, and it has a faint yellow-brown patch on the shoulder. How can I rescue it?

A Depends on how bad the mark is: if it's a light singe you might be able to fade it with regular washing. Add an in-wash stain remover to boost your detergent, or soak the shirt in a solution of 1 tablespoon washing soda to 500ml warm water for a few hours before washing as normal. If this doesn't work, try bleaching the stain by rubbing it with lemon juice, cover with salt and leave for at least an hour before rinsing and washing as normal.

Still there? Then I'm afraid your shirt's destined for the recycling bin.

Q When I iron shirts and blouses, there's often a faint sweaty smell over the armpit area. I've tried adding disinfectant to the wash but nothing changes. What should I do?

A Wash the shirts at the hottest temperature the fabric allows and, provided they're colourfast, in a detergent with bleach. You'll need to up the dosage if you're in a hard-water area (you can tell by looking inside your kettle: a fur coat on the heating element is a definite sign). Powdered detergent is best, because the dosage can be adjusted to the size of the washload, level of soiling and water type.

Use a fabric conditioner to help ensure any smells from the wash are pleasant, and don't overload the machine – you should be able to place your hand comfortably on top of the load and see a section of the drum at the back. When the cycle is finished, remove the clothes immediately and dry outdoors if possible.

For ironing, fill the water tank with scented water, such as Comfort Vaporesse (from supermarkets), instead of tap water (but check the iron instructions first). This should inject extra freshness and mask any lingering armpit pongs.

If none of this works, try pre-treating the underarms with White Wizard, £4.88 for 283g from Lakeland (01539 488100, www.lakeland.co.uk).

Q I have a problem with black gunge growing around my washing machine's soap dispenser. Despite cleaning it with bleach, it persists. What can I do?

A The gunge is mould. Don't use bleach – it could damage rubber parts inside the machine. Instead, remove the drawer and use Milton Sterilising Fluid from supermarkets. Dilute according to instructions and use a nylon brush to scrub before leaving to soak for a few minutes. Wipe inside the housing of the drawer with the solution too. This may not stop the mould reappearing, since inside the machine is damp, but leaving the door open to allow air to circulate will help.

Q I set my washing machine to run at a hotter programme than I intended and the dye from one item has coloured the rest of the load. Is there any way to fix this?

A You need to use a bleach-free colour run remover that won't affect the original colours. Try either Dylon Colour Run Remover, or Dr. Beckmann Colour Run Remover. These can be used either in the machine or in a handwash (leave to soak for up to an hour, then wash as normal).

From now on when you do a mixed colour wash, put a Colour Catcher sheet in the drum and add detergent. It acts as a magnet, catching any loose dye and grime. All of these products are available from most supermarkets.

Q Rust-like stains keeping appearing on clothes coming out of the washing machine. What's going on and how do I get rid of the marks?

A They're probably iron mould, which grows if rusty marks are left untreated. It's unusual for the machine itself to be the cause; more likely it's something like a stray bra wire, coin or a screw left in a pocket that gets trapped between the drums and goes rusty. These bits and pieces work themselves through the holes of the drum or between the drum and door seal. A few tips:

✳ Check the filter and inside the fold of the rubber seal around the door – odds and sods can collect here.

✳ Inspect the holes inside the drum – you might detect a screw or bra wire sticking out of one of the holes and you can pull it through. If you can't see anything, wrap a nylon stocking around a cloth and rub it over the surface – the stocking will snag if it comes across anything sharp.

If you think there may be foreign metal objects inside and you can't get to them, you need to call out an engineer to dismantle the machine and remove whatever is there.

The other reason could be iron in the water. Roadworks, heavy rainfall or drought can bring on conditions that cause contamination (which could explain why the staining is sporadic). There's little you can do except wait for the water to return to normal. Check the supply by running tap water through a white cloth for five minutes. If iron is present, you'll see it.

To treat the stains, you'll probably find that light marks won't need special treatment – just wash as you normally would. If nothing changes, try rubbing with lots of lemon juice, cover with salt and leave a few hours. Rinse and wash as normal. Iron mould transfers easily from one garment to another, so you should treat affected clothes straight away.

Q My washing machine has black mould on the grey concertina rubber ring, which is impossible to shift. I leave the door open when not in use and have it on most days.
A This is a very common problem, usually caused by constantly washing at 40°C or below or only using the quick wash. Low temperatures won't kill the bacteria on your washing, so when the water drains away, the bacteria is left behind to build up inside the machine. Your machine will start to smell and soon afterwards black mould will begin to make an appearance on the seal. In extreme cases, you will also notice black/grey

round marks on your clothes. (Rewashing at the hottest temperature the fabric will allow, in biological detergent, should remove them.) It's important to deal with it quickly as mould can corrode the door seal and pipes.

You need to do a 'maintenance wash': run the empty machine on the hottest wash possible with a cup of clear vinegar. You may have to repeat three or four times if the problem is really bad. Try to do at least one wash at 60°C or more each week.

Q My tumble-dryer has had its day and I want to be environmentally friendly and not replace it. Where can I buy a traditional clothes dryer that hangs from the ceiling?

A Several places stock these, including Lakeland: the Traditional Airer, £50.24 inc p&p by mail order only (01539 488100; www.lakeland.co.uk), is 1.8m long (although you could cut it down if you want) and comes with cast-iron fixings, pulleys and four pine rails. Alternatively, The Domestic Paraphernalia Company (0800 9774002; www.dpcompany.co.uk) sells the original Sheila Maid, which has been around forever. It also has cast-iron fixings, pulleys and four pine rails (there's a six-rail version too) and comes in four sizes (1.45m up to 2.44m), while the rack ends are available in six colours. Prices start at £59.50 inc p&p for a coloured 1.45m airer. Spare parts are available from both companies.

Q I got caught in the rain wearing my new velvet jacket, which is now covered in spots. Brushing makes no difference – what can I do?

A You can get it looking new again – but it'll take time and a lot of patience. Start by placing it on the ironing board. Wet a clothes brush (just enough to make the jacket feel damp) and gently brush a section of the velvet in the direction of the nap. It'll look awful, but worry not. Leave to dry overnight away from direct heat but still on the ironing board: don't move it! Then take a dry brush over it, first against the nap, then in the direction of the nap. Now move on to the next section, but don't get any water or fingerprints on the panel you've just treated. Keep going until you've done the whole jacket – it could take a week, but if you want it restored to its spotless state, it's the only way. Now treat with a protector spray before you wear it outside again!

Q My daughter lent her friend a crinkly black top made of polyester with the label: 'Handwash in cold water, do not iron'. The friend handwashed but also ironed it, and the crinkly bits have been smoothed out. Any way back?

A The crinkles are made by crushing the fabric and applying controlled heat, but the heat of the iron softened the fibres and smoothed out the wrinkles. So try ironing the top again along the original principles. There's a risk that you could melt the polyester, so take care. Start by laying a clean white sheet over your ironing board, place the top over it, scrunch it up to try to realign the wrinkles and cover with another clean white sheet. This will help protect the fibres from melting or becoming glazed by the heat and pressure of the iron. Then, with your iron on a three-dot setting (without steam), press firmly over the sheet and hold in place for 30 seconds. Don't move it backwards and forwards. Leave to cool for a few seconds before moving on to the next area. Good luck.

Furniture

Q I stupidly used my wooden dining table for ironing, and the impression of my lacy tablecloth has burnt on to the table. Help!

A If the surface hasn't roughened you may be able to fix it with a cream metal polish rubbed briskly in the direction of the grain, followed by a light rubbing with wax polish. Or get Liberon Ring Remover (01797 367555 for stockists). Test on a hidden area first and work in small sections, wiping away the cream often to check progress.

If the surface is rough to touch, the wood is damaged. If this is the case, use very fine steel wool dipped in liquid wax polish, again working in the direction of the grain. Take huge care on veneered finishes.

For more serious burns, you'll need to get professional help. Contact either the Association of Master Upholsterers

& Soft Furnishers (029 20778918, www.upholsterers.co.uk) or the British Antique Furniture Restorers' Association (01305 854822, www.bafra.org.uk) for local companies.

Q There's a greasy mark on my husband's side of our wooden headboard. How do I get rid of this?

A You need to treat the whole board, otherwise you'll end up with patchiness. Wash down with a cloth soaked in a warm solution of mild soapflakes and a little lemon juice, taking care not to overwet. No need to rinse – just buff dry with a soft cloth. If it still looks grubby, get Bald's Original Furniture Balm from John Lewis (08456 049049) or Lakeland (01539 488100; www.lakeland.co.uk). There are two types: green top for light woods and red for dark (if in doubt, go for green) and they can be used on both lacquered and waxed furniture (you won't need to re-wax). It's made from a blend of natural oils and works by gently cleaning the stain and putting oils back into the wood, which will help protect the surface. You might need more than one application but it smells bracingly beautiful. Apply sparingly with a soft cloth or brush (good for mouldings or awkward corners) in the direction of the grain before wiping with a clean cloth to remove any surplus.

Q How can I remove a white ring, made by a hot cup, on a polished pine surface?

A Check the surface: if it's not roughened, put a dab of cream metal polish such as Brasso on a duster and rub the mark briskly in the direction of the grain. Then polish lightly with a normal wax polish (not a spray). Otherwise get Liberon Ring Remover (call 01797 367555 for stockists), which works in a similar way. Whichever method you use, always test on a hidden area first and work in small sections at a time, wiping away the cream often to check progress.

If the surface is rough, the finish of the wood has been damaged. In this case, try smoothing over the surface by rubbing very fine steel wool dipped in liquid wax polish, again working in the direction of the grain. But take care: this method should be used with extreme caution on veneered finishes.

If you don't want to risk doing it yourself (or if the table is valuable), contact either the Association of Master Upholsterers & Soft Furnishers (029 20778918, www.upholsterers.co.uk) or the British Antique Furniture Restorers' Association (01305 854822, www.bafra.org.uk) for companies in your area. Incidentally, all the above methods can be used to remove ring marks caused by wet glasses, vases or plant pots.

Q My pine cupboard has darkened over the years, even though it's out of direct sunlight. It's large and overpowering and used to be quite handsome – is there any way I can lighten it without painting?

A All timber will darken a bit, although it's more noticeable with lighter-coloured, soft woods such as pine. It's caused by the sun reacting with the resins in the wood, much as a newspaper yellows, and it happens regardless of the finish (although some

TOP TIP

How to keep your antique furniture looking its best...

First the good news: you need to polish most items only once or twice a year (dining tables in daily use are perhaps the only exception), otherwise the polish will build up, making the surface sticky and prone to attracting dirt. Check by running your fingers across the surface: if it smears, you're using too much polish.

For everyday dusting, wipe over with a barely damp duster and buff dry to revive the shine. Remove sticky marks with a cloth wrung out in a warm, mild soap-flake solution (Dri-Pak Soap Flakes or Dri-Pak Pure Liquid Soap from hardware stores or supermarkets), taking care not to over-wet. No need to rinse, just dry with a soft cloth.

Never use spray polish or brands with added silicones. Yes, they give instant shine, but the film doesn't fill in scratches or blemishes the way wax-based products do. More importantly, solvents in the spray can soften underlying layers of wax and, if used too often, make the surface sticky (and sometimes cause it to turn milky, for which there's no cure, short of stripping and resurfacing).

Beeswax-based polishes are the best, but apply sparingly. If you put too much on it will dry before you have finished, leaving the surface smeary and difficult to buff.

Solid wax gives the best shine, but needs more effort. Allow the wax to dry for a few minutes before buffing to achieve a better shine (and it'll be less effort, always a good thing).

Lastly, if the dye in the polish is darker than the wood, it will darken it. If you use a lighter-coloured polish on dark wood, ensure that no residue is left in the crevices.

lacquers have built-in UV protectors that slow down the process). It doesn't have to be in direct sunlight either: furniture will show some colour change in a north-facing room within two years (it can be as quick as a month if it's south-facing). The only way to lighten it is to remove the old finish, sand down to the natural wood and start again. You can do this yourself, but it's a long, hard job and you'll probably get better results if you have it done professionally, particularly as it's such a large piece. FIRA International (01438 777700; www.askfira.co.uk) can give you details of companies in your area.

Q I put a church candle in a large saucer on our lovely Georgian mahogany table, but it spat, and about six inches of wax ran on to the table. I picked some of it off gently when cold, but the rest is stuck. What can I do?
A First thing to do is fill a plastic bag with ice cubes and place it over the area for a few minutes. This will harden the wax

and make it easier to chip away gently with a plastic scraper. After you've got rid of all the wax, remove any remaining film with a duster, and polish as normal. If heat marking shows (usually as a white bloom), rub briskly along the grain with a metal polish.

Q I have a 40-year-old camphor-wood-lined, carved, unlacquered teak chest from Singapore. It is ingrained with dirt, which has been polished over, and now it looks terrible. How can I clean it?

A Liberon Wax and Polish Remover (call 01797 367555 for stockists) will remove all the old layers of wax and ingrained dirt. The makers assure me it won't affect the original finish. Apply with a small pad of very fine grade wire wool. Rub gently in the direction of the grain, in small areas at a time, and wipe off the dirt with a clean cloth as you go. Allow to dry thoroughly. The surface will look a bit dull, but don't worry. You're now ready to re-wax the chest using a clear, hard wax such as Antiquax Original Wax Polish, from hardware stores. Never use a spray polish. Apply sparingly and buff like mad! The secret is to build up three to four thin layers of wax, buffing in between; a clean, soft shoe-brush is ideal, especially in the carved areas. To keep it looking good, dust regularly with a barely damp duster and buff dry. Polish every six months, making sure you first remove any dust.

Q **I bought a lovely Victorian pine chest for bed linen, but the wood is impregnated with the smell of mothballs. What can I do?**

A It's difficult, because this pungent smell really gets into the wood, but it will gradually fade over time (although bear in mind that this may take anything up to a year). In the meantime, try airing the chest by leaving the drawers open and washing it with a damp cloth wrung out in warm soapy water (make sure not to over-wet, though). Rinse and allow to dry. Next put in some air fresheners and keep the empty drawers shut for a few weeks. You can make your own by putting 3 tablespoons of bicarbonate of soda into a bowl and then adding a few drops of your favourite essential oil – lavender's lovely.

Q **I've inherited a walnut sideboard from my grandmother, which has been zealously spray-polished over the past 44 years. The surface is sticky with a build-up of polish. How can I safely (and easily) remove this?**

A Sounds as if your grandmother may have been using the wrong polish. You need to strip and resurface.

First, remove the build-up with something like Rustin's Surface Cleaner from hardware stores (or call **020 84504666** for stockists). Apply with a soft cloth (or, if the wood is very dirty, with extra fine steel wool), wiping off the solution with a soft clean rag or kitchen roll. Otherwise use white spirit, but only if the sideboard has a wax finish – white spirit will damage a lacquered surface, so first test on a small area.

You're now ready to re-polish with a wax paste. If the sideboard is antique or valuable, you should have it restored professionally. Contact the British Antique Furniture Restorers' Association (01305 854822, www.bafra.org.uk) for companies in your area.

Once your sideboard is restored, you need only use a wax polish once, or at most, twice a year. Solid wax, as opposed to a cream, definitely gives the best results, but it does need a lot of elbow grease.

Q **My cream-coloured wicker table and chairs, housed in the dampish conservatory, have developed a covering of grey mould in some places. I've had a good scrub to try to get rid of it, but without success. What can I do?**

A Cane furniture normally has a light varnish and you just wipe it down with water to keep it clean. For heavier dirt you'd use a mild solution of washing-up liquid – anything harsher might break through the varnish and damage the cane underneath. Sounds like you're beyond that. My advice now would be to stain your furniture with a darkish varnish to hide the marks. Rustin's does a range of wood-care products; if you ring them on 020 8450 4666 (ask for the technical department) and tell them what sort of finish you're looking for, they'll advise you what to buy.

Q **We have a cream wicker (or rattan?) four-piece suite that's looking grubby. How should we clean it? We'd also like to change the colour to pale pink – advice, please!**

A Sounds as if it could be made of cane, rattan, willow or bamboo, but most have a varnish or sealer for protection, so vacuuming with an upholstery nozzle and wiping with a damp cloth should do it. For heavier dirt, you'll need to wash with a solution of washing-up liquid; don't use anything harsher as it may break the seal and damage the cane underneath. You need to work on a warm, sunny day so that it dries quickly, otherwise it can go mouldy. Use a clean soft shoe-brush on the surface, then rinse and allow to dry naturally away from direct heat.

Once clean and dry, you can get down to colouring it. Use two or three light coats of spray paint, such as Plasti-kote Super Spray Paint, from DIY stores (not ordinary paints or brush, as they'll clog up the weave). It's available in 60 colours (including your pale pink), gloss, satin and matt, there's no pre-sanding and it's touch-dry within 50 minutes. For best results use a primer first, such as Plasti-kote Super Primer. As the paint needs to blow through the weave, it's definitely a job to do outdoors. If you don't feel up to it, Cane & Rush Restoration (01494 452453) can do the work from around £360. They cover London and offer a pick-up service within a 30-mile radius of West Wycombe; otherwise you need to get the furniture to and from the shop.

Q I tried to clean the arms of my Dralon sofa using the upholstery attachment of a steam cleaner. They're certainly clean, but the pile is badly crushed. How can I raise it again?

A Not good news: the intense heat generated by the steam cleaner will have distorted the pile and set it into a new position… and it's impossible to get it back to how it was. You'll either have to live with it (maybe get some arm covers?) or buy a new sofa. Either way, check with your insurance company to see if you're covered for accidental damage.

Q My leather suite has marks from people's greasy heads. What can I do?

A Tricky, as the grease gets absorbed by the leather and, as a rule, you can only clean stains off the surface of leather and not out of it; once inside, it's a specialist job. Leave the grime to build up and the leather will crack and disintegrate. If it's superficial, you may be able to break down the grease with a cleaner such as LTT Leather Shampoo, £12.50 for 200ml inc p&p from LTT Leather Care (01423 881027; www.lttleather-care.co.uk). Apply with a sponge and wipe the whole panel gently before removing the foam with a paper towel. If this doesn't work, it'll need professional restoration. It's not cheap: expect to pay around £250 for a chair and £450 for a sofa. The suite will be at the workshop for around 10 days. The process involves degreasing with a powder to draw out the body oils. This also removes colour and finish, so it has to be reapplied by hand. Contact LTT Leather Care (as above) for firms in your area.

To keep furniture looking good, use LTT La..zy Leather, £15.50 for 250ml inc p&p (as above) every two to four weeks (even if it doesn't seem dirty). Pay attention to body-contact areas. Then treat twice yearly with a leather protector such as LTT Leather Protect, £15.50 for 150ml inc p&p (as above). For more advice visit the LTT website.

Q I've been given a couple of chairs upholstered in short, velvet-like pile. One of the seats has an indentation where a computer was sitting. How can I remove this?
A Sometimes the marks can be teased out with a weak solution of fabric softener and lukewarm water (two or three drops of softener to 3 litres water). Apply to the fibres using a small sponge, taking care not to over-wet, then gently stroke the surface with a folded towel to try to lift and realign the pile. Rinse with water, blotting often with kitchen towel, and remove as much moisture as you can by blotting with a towel or using a hairdryer on a cool setting. Finally, set the pile in a uniform direction and leave to dry.

Q How can I remove denim dye from a cream leather sofa?
A The denim has effectively re-dyed the leather – known as 'dye transfer'. The fault lies with the clothing rather than the leather; dye loss from jeans should reduce with every wash. But you need to act quickly: the longer it's left, the deeper it'll go into the surface and the harder it'll be to remove.

So, depending on how big the stain is and how long it's been there, you might be lucky in cleaning it off with a good-quality leather cleaner such as LTT La..zy Leather, £15.50 for 250ml inc p&p from LTT Leather Care (01423 881027; www. lttleathercare.co.uk). Spray on to the leather and wipe the whole panel gently with a soft cloth. You should start to see the dye residue lifting on to the cloth. Repeat if necessary. If that doesn't work, try LTT Maxi Cleaner, £15 for 200ml inc p&p (as above). This is slightly stronger and specifically formulated for dye transfer, so if this fails, it's time to have your sofa cleaned professionally. Contact LTT Leather Care for firms in your area.

All light-coloured leathers are prone to show dye transfer, but if cleaned every fortnight and protected twice-yearly, you can reduce the risk. Try LTT Leather Protect, £15.50 for 150ml inc p&p (as above). For more advice visit the website.

Q My bedroom has fitted wardrobes that back on to an exterior wall. There's no ventilation and my clothes suffer from mildew marking. Is there a way around this?
A Any structural damp problems you'll need to sort, otherwise the mildew will always be there. Then treat the inside of the external wall with Polycell Damp Seal (0870 4441111; www.polycell.co.uk) – a specially formulated paint that seals patches of penetrating damp and stops them coming through. It's a one-off treatment, and you need only one coat: apply generously with a brush (I'd treat the whole wall), paying particular attention to problem areas. Allow to dry overnight before redecorating with your own paint or wallpaper.

If any stains show through, spray with Polycell Stain Stop – stockists as above – before repainting the wall.

Q I have a Lloyd Loom ottoman, which I use for linen and some wedding gifts from 1962. Small rust-coloured marks have spread throughout the bottom half of the piece and some items are smothered in places. What's happened, and how can I rescue the linen?

A Sounds as if your ottoman has developed iron mould. Lloyd Loom furniture is made from twisted paper and wire, and it has probably become damp at some stage (maybe you put away some slightly damp linen after washing?). This has rusted the wire, which has spread to your linen to form iron mould. Iron mould is easily transferred, so you need to treat affected items as quickly as possible.

For light rust marks on your machine-washable linens, wash as normal. If the stains won't shift, rub with lemon juice, cover with salt and leave for a good hour. Rinse and wash as normal. If you have anything precious or very delicate, such as lace or satin, you might be better giving it to a specialist dry cleaner.

And before you put your newly revived linens back into the ottoman, you'll need to paint both inside and out to seal the rust – easiest with a can of car spray paint (not ordinary decorating paints or a brush, as they'll clog up the weave). Use the appropriate undercoat spray paint first. And, bearing in mind you need to allow the paint to blow through the weave, it's definitely a job to do outdoors.

Q I have a beautiful brass table with a detailed pattern that I like to keep shiny. But no matter how I clean it,

Brasso gets stuck in the pattern. I've tried everything – toothbrush, washing, a pointy knife – all in vain. Any suggestions?

A Try a towel dampened with paraffin – it's a great de-greaser and should shift those annoyances. Rub over the surface and use a baby's toothbrush for getting into deeper crevices. Wipe with a clean, lint-free cloth. You now have several options.

First, you could switch to another polish. Town Talk's Brass & Copper Polish, £5.28 for 250ml inc p&p (01204 520014), dries to a powder and is less likely to leave a residue. Apply sparingly and buff with a clean, dry cloth.

In between polishing and when dusting, use an impregnated polishing cloth like Town Talk's Gold Polishing Cloth (fine for brass), £4.46 (30 x 45cm) inc p&p, also available as a pair of mitts (lined with cloth to keep your hands clean), £7.28 inc p&p. Stockist as above.

But what about stopping polishing altogether? You could apply a few coats of Renaissance Micro-Crystalline Wax Polish, £11.50 for 200ml inc p&p (020 8202 8972; www.picreator. co.uk). Formulated in the British Museum research lab, it'll protect your table from dirt and grease and stop it re-tarnishing. Apply about three thin layers, allowing the first to dry before building up. Buff with a soft cloth as you go to give a lustrous finish. You should then only need to reapply annually. Between times, dust with a soft dry cloth. To remove greasy fingermarks, wipe with your paraffin-dampened rag and buff dry with a soft, lint-free cloth.

Q The tops and sides of our piano's ivory keys have years of grime. How should I clean them?

A Not with water – ivory is porous and eventually it will lose its shine and become rough. Instead, rub the keys with a little meths, taking care not to get any on the piano case, then buff them dry with a lint-free cloth. Don't use meths on the black keys – it's not always easy to tell if they're ebony or another polished wood, and the meths would strip the polish. (If a little gets on them, wipe quickly with a clean duster.) Since the black keys don't show up the dirt as much anyway, clean them with a bit of spit (honestly!), then buff dry.

Ivory is naturally yellow; it's bleached during manufacture, but can discolour with age and use, and bad discoloration needs professional sanding and polishing. If you want to sort this, look in the *Yellow Pages* under 'piano tuning and repairs'.

Modern pianos have plastic-coated keys and don't discolour in the same way. Just dust regularly, clean any marks with a damp cloth and buff dry.

Housework is something you do
that no one notices until you don't do it
─────
Anon

Flooring

Q I need to get my carpets cleaned. Is this something I could do myself? What are the different options available, the relative costs involved and the pros and cons?

A You can either clean your carpets yourself – by buying a machine or hiring one, such as from the Rug Doctor, around £19.99 for 24 hours plus shampoo (01903 235558; www.rugdoctor.co.uk) – or you can have it done professionally. A DIY job is cheaper, but hard work. If you have children and/or pets, it may be worth buying your own 3-in-1 machine, such as the Vax 6131, around £145 (0870 6061248; www.vax.co.uk).

But I think carpet cleaning is best done by the professionals; they have specialist solutions, more powerful machines, and they do the hard work (always a bonus in my book). There are several methods, including shampooing or bonnet-buffing (detergent is worked into the carpet with a spinning mop or rotary brush); hot water extraction (the carpet is pre-sprayed with a heated detergent solution before being rinsed and the dirt sucked out); dry-powder cleaning (absorbent powders impregnated with cleaning agents are worked into the carpet before being vacuumed away); and a hot-carbonating extraction system (unique to Chem-Dry: they use a naturally-based solution and a special carbonating process to create millions of tiny bubbles that lift the dirt and allergens to the surface for extraction).

Which to choose? Each has pluses and minuses: shampooing takes longest to dry (times vary with carpet type, level of dirt and weather), whereas dry-powder cleaning is fast to dry but suitable only for light soiling.

The most important thing is to find a good company – any decent carpet cleaner will offer various methods. He should not be quoting a price until he's assessed the area, condition, age and level of dirt, which will determine the most appropriate cleaning method (hence it's impossible for me to give a price guide). Whoever you choose, use either a member of the National Carpet Cleaners Association (0116 2719550, www.ncca.co.uk) or contact Chem-Dry (01482 872770; www.chemdry.co.uk) direct.

Q **I have food stains on my dining-room carpet that I have removed twice with Vanish, only for them to reappear afterwards. Any solutions?**

A The stains are probably grease-based and you haven't managed to remove all the grease. You may have pushed the stain further in while cleaning, or you didn't clean thoroughly enough. Either way, grease is working its way back to the surface. It's also possible that you haven't rinsed the carpet properly and the residue is attracting dirt.

So let's start again! The first step in cleaning mystery stains is to treat them as oil/grease-based. Gently dab with white spirit on a paper towel (test on a hidden area first) – if it's grease, you'll see it on the towel and the stain will fade. Continue until all is gone; no need to rinse. However, if traces remain, or if nothing shifts, treat it as a water-based stain and use a weak detergent solution: mix 1 teaspoon Woolite or the like to 300ml warm water. Work from the outer edge of the stain inwards, using a little at a time, and blot often with paper towel. Keep wetting and blotting until the stain goes. Do the same with clean water to rinse thoroughly and don't rub. Finally, place several sheets of paper towel on top, weigh down with heavy books, and leave overnight. This will help absorb any stain that has penetrated to the backing. Once dry, vacuum to restore a fluffy pile.

Q How can I get black bicycle oil stains out of my living-room carpet? I've used various products I had lying around the house, to no avail.
A Now try 1001 Troubleshooter, from supermarkets. Work from the outside edge of the stain in, using a clean damp cloth

> **TOP TIP**
> *How to remove trodden-in Blu-Tack from a carpet...*
>
> Try holding a plastic bottle filled with hot water over the area – it'll soften the Blu-Tack and you should be able to pull it away by dabbing it with sticky tape (or a fresh chunk of Blu-Tack). If that doesn't work, try teasing it from the carpet fibres with a comb or pin. For more deeply ingrained stains, you'll also need a stain remover such as Dr. Beckmann Stain Slayer, from supermarkets or online at www.dr-beckmann.co.uk.

and a blotting action (if you rub too much the carpet will fuzz). Blot excess moisture with kitchen paper and vacuum when completely dry.

If that doesn't do it, use Dr. Beckmann Stain Slayer, from supermarkets or online at www.dr-beckmann.co.uk. It's a good multi-purpose stain remover for clothes, carpets and upholstery, and it sounds as if, with your mucky habits, it'll always come in handy!

Test on a discreet area first for colour fastness and allow to dry completely before you go ahead. And keep that bike outside in future.

Q After I spilt candle wax on a new carpet, I left it to dry, then set about removing it with brown paper and a warm iron. I mistakenly turned the dial to hot, the brown paper stuck to the carpet and the surrounding area is now stiff and discoloured (but not scorched). What now?

A If the mark is light, you might get away with trimming the tufts with a small pair of very sharp scissors. If it's gone beyond that, you'll be able to fade the mark but not totally get rid of it. Use a stiff brush to remove loose fibres and bits of brown paper, then gently rub a piece of very fine sandpaper in a circular motion over the mark. Don't over-rub, otherwise you might end up with a frizzy mess.

Q Our Flotex kitchen carpet badly needs cleaning. It's laid on non-marine hardboard so I daren't allow it to get too wet and don't think my Vax shampooer would be suitable. What's the best solution?

A It's fine to use your Vax shampooer (a 3-in-1 machine). Flotex has a PVC backing so it's waterproof, although you should take care not to over-wet it if there are seams. Use the detergent supplied with your Vax, but a very weak solution: about one part detergent to 100 parts water. Then rinse the floor well with clear water and leave to dry. If you need any further information, contact Flotex on 0800 0282161; www.flotex.co.uk.

Q Help! I've spilt some Copydex glue on the carpet. How should I deal with it?

A Loosen the dried bits of glue with an eraser and pick them off with your fingers. Treat any stain left behind by dabbing with a weak detergent solution (1 teaspoon of detergent for washing woollens to 300ml warm water), taking care not to over-wet. Rinse well and blot dry.

Q There's an old bloodstain on my wool/nylon light fawn carpet. What's the best way to remove it?

A Hate to say it, but these can be hell to shift. You should really dab a bloodstain while it's fresh, with a white towel, then sponge with cold water and blot dry (never use hot as it could set the blood). So what you need to do now is try a carpet stain remover such as 1001 Spot Shot for Carpets, from DIY stores. You might need to apply it a few times, so be patient.

Otherwise try this homemade remedy. Start by sponging the stain with a solution of 1 teaspoon of detergent for washing woollens to 300ml warm water. Work inwards from the outside edge of the stain, using a little at a time, and blot frequently with either a white towel or kitchen paper. Then do the same with an ammonia solution – 1 teaspoon of household ammonia (from hardware stores) to one cupful of warm water. Blot dry.

Finally, spray with a solution of one part clear vinegar to four parts water. Blot (don't rub) to soak up excess moisture. When dry, run the vacuum cleaner over the carpet to restore the fluffy pile.

If this doesn't work, it's over to the professionals.

Q While cleaning a stain on our beige carpet, my husband put a greasy washing-up bowl on it, which left an even worse stain! Professional steam cleaning hasn't worked: it keeps reappearing. Any ideas?

A I don't hold out much hope since you've had it professionally cleaned, but you could try fuller's earth from LTP (01823 666213; www.ltp-online.co.uk). Put some over the stain, rub it in gently and leave a couple of days before vacuuming.

Q A visiting friend has left a large henna stain on my carpet. How do I get it out?

A Depends on what type of carpet it is. With a synthetic pile, the dye won't penetrate the fibres, so you should be able to remove it by gently dabbing with a simple detergent solution (1 teaspoon Woolite to 300ml warm water). Work from the outside in and avoid scrubbing as this may create a larger stain and go deeper into the pile. Repeat until no more colour is lifted. Finish by rinsing with plenty of clean water, then blot dry with paper towels.

With a natural wool carpet, the dye is likely to penetrate the fibres and colour them in the same way as hair. So start with the method as above, and if that doesn't work, try a solution of vitamin C (one tablet dissolved in a teaspoon of water – you only need to dab a small amount on the stain). The theory is that the vitamin C breaks down the molecules in the dye and should fade the stain. Test a hidden area first to ensure you don't fade the colour or damage the pile. Finish by rinsing with clean water and blot dry with paper towels.

Q My four-year-old granddaughter has trodden deep red lipstick into my beige carpet. How on earth do I clean it?

A Hmm, tricky, but if you are extremely patient you can get it out. Lipstick is a complex stain containing both grease and highly coloured pigments. You need to dissolve the greasy part first, then deal with the dye.

Start by very gently scraping off any lumpy bits with a blunt knife, taking care not to spread the stain. Then squirt on a few drops of WD-40, wait a few seconds, then blot with paper towel. Work from the outside inwards, using a delicate dabbing motion. You must be careful to avoid pushing the stain deeper into the carpet or spreading it. Repeat until no more colour is lifted.

Next stage: remove any remaining traces with White Wizard, from Lakeland (01539 488100; www.lakeland.co.uk). Apply to the mark and leave for a minute, then blot with lightly dampened kitchen paper or a clean white towel. Dab the area with clean water to rinse, then blot dry. Repeat until the stain is removed.

Q When decorating my picture rail with Dulux Black Eggshell Wood paint I dripped a little on my cream-coloured carpet. How can I get it off?

A Oops – the Dulux people tell me this is difficult to remove once dry – you need to treat it immediately. However, they said that if the stain is still soft underneath (even though it may be dry to the touch), you might be able to fade the mark by dabbing it with white spirit. Test a hidden area first in case it affects the carpet colour, then rinse and blot dry immediately after treating. If this doesn't work it's a professional job: contact the National Carpet Cleaners Association (0116 2719550, www.ncca.co.uk), who'll give you details of members in your area.

Q How can I get pine tree resin out of my carpet? It must have fallen off when we brought our potted living tree in for Christmas. I tried tar remover without success, then meths, which has removed only some of the dirt.

A Keep on with the meths, but don't over-wet the carpet. Use a small amount and dab it on to the fibre tips with cotton wool. Then place a sheet of kitchen paper over the top and massage with the underside of a spoon. Keep moving the paper until all the meths is absorbed. Repeat if necessary, but leave a few minutes between applications to allow the meths to evaporate. Finally, clean the area with a mild detergent solution(1 teaspoon of detergent for woollens to 300ml warm water), rinse well and blot dry. If this doesn't work, contact the National Carpet Cleaners Association (0116 2719550; www.ncca.co.uk), who will give you details of members in your area.

Q A friend spilled black ink on our cream carpet while changing the inkjet printer cartridge. He covered the stain with a box and now it's set in. Help!

A Your so-called friend should have rinsed the area with cold water straight away. You could now try washing it with a sudsy household ammonia and cold water solution. Work from the outer edge inwards, taking care not to over-wet. Blot with kitchen paper. Rinse with cold water and blot dry. Still no luck? Then it's over to the professionals.

Q My bedroom radiator, with verdigris on the pipes, leaked on to my pale carpet, leaving a nasty green stain. I've tried carpet cleaner, but to no effect. Any other suggestions?

A Try using Magica Rust Remover, £11.50 inc p&p from Kitchen Economy (029 20451222), safe on most surfaces except glass and ceramic. Spray on to the affected area – you don't have to rub – and rinse off with water. If the stain is bad, you may have to repeat. And if it doesn't disappear, then it probably isn't rust. Always test on a discreet area first for colour fastness. And get those pipes sorted!

Q My carpet has rust stains from castors on a chair, replaced when the carpet was still damp after shampooing. Household carpet shampoo has no effect. What to do?

A Try Magica Rust Remover, £11.50 inc p&p, from Kitchen Economy (029 20451222) – it may take several goes. Spray it on – don't rub – and rinse well with water. Blot dry. Test a hidden area first, and wear rubber gloves. Still no joy? Call in a member of the National Carpet Cleaners Association (0116 2719550, www.ncca.co.uk).

In future, if you shampoo the carpet yourself, place a small piece of kitchen foil under the feet of furniture, and ensure the carpet is absolutely dry before removing (minimum 24 hours).

Q A visitor's polished shoes have left marks on my light coloured woollen-mix carpet. How can I clean them off?
A Squirt a few drops of WD-40 on the marks, wait 30 seconds, then blot with white kitchen paper, moving to clean areas of the paper all the time. Work from the outside in, dabbing very gently to avoid pushing the stain in more deeply or spreading it. Repeat until no more of the stain is coming up. Remove any remaining traces of colour with White Wizard from Lakeland (01539 488100; www.lakeland.co.uk). Apply and leave for a minute or so, then blot with a clean damp white cloth. Finish by dabbing the area with clean water to rinse, then blot dry. You might need to do this a few times.

Q While decorating my stairway I used wide Sellotape instead of masking tape to stick newspaper to the carpet. I've removed the tape but the residue has stuck to the carpet and is collecting dirt. Help!
A Try dabbing with meths, then use a damp cloth to remove the residue, and follow up with a carpet shampoo. Or use Mykal Sticky Stuff Remover from John Lewis, Focus and Wilkinson. Apply a little with a clean dry cloth; leave for a few

minutes before blotting with kitchen paper. Take care on foam- or rubber-backed carpets: don't let the liquid seep into the backing otherwise you could end up dissolving the glue fixing the backing. Clean afterwards with carpet shampoo.

Q My lovely Indian silk rug has had some candle wax spilled on it. I removed what I could but am left with two stains that ruin the rug's look and feel. Any suggestions?
A Two things to try. The 'cold' way: fill a plastic bag with ice cubes and place over the wax till it goes really brittle. Pick off the residue using a blunt knife blade or your fingernail.

The 'hot' method is to put a few sheets of absorbent kitchen paper over the area and gently press with a warm, dry iron, moving the paper until the wax has been absorbed. Take care not to let the iron touch the rug as it could scorch it – and that's a whole other Q and A!

If the rug is still stained at this stage, dab lightly with meths, but test on a hidden area first as it could cause discoloration.

Q My friend and I each brought home a sheepskin rug from holiday. She took hers to the dry cleaner and it lost its softness and shine. I don't want to ruin mine – what do you recommend?
A If it was expensive the skin was probably chrome tanned when cured. This gives the skin a bluey-greyness on the under-side, but it depends on the type and which animal it's from. If you can be absolutely sure, you should be able to handwash it,

but it's not easy. Do it in the bath using a neutral detergent such as washing-up liquid (not washing powder as it's too alkaline and will do damage) and make sure you rinse and dry thoroughly. Whatever you do, *do not* machine wash!

If the rug was a cheapie, it'll probably have been vegetable tanned. The back usually has a creamy yellow appearance (but again depending on the skin type and age). These can't be washed as they tend to dry out and go hard.

Best bet is to have it dry cleaned too, but make sure you use a cleaner used to working with suede and leather. They will re-oil the rug to replace the natural oils removed during cleaning (something your friend's dry cleaner probably didn't do). Contact the Textile Services Association (020 8863 7755; www.tsa-uk.org) for members.

And don't clean the rug too often or it'll curl at the edges.

Q My husband spilt a bowl of cereal on a rug brought back from the Middle East. I washed it with water, but now it has dried, that area is stiff and dark. What can I do?

A Despite your best attempts, it sounds as if you've not removed all the milk, which is why the patch is stiffer and darker. You did right to clean the carpet with water, but now you need to clean the patch again using a detergent solution – 1 teaspoon of gentle detergent for washing woollens to 300ml of warm water. Work from the outer edge of the stain inwards, using a little solution at a time and blotting up all the time with kitchen paper. Then do the same with an ammonia solution –

1 teaspoon of household ammonia (from hardware stores) to 1 cupful of warm water. Blot dry. Finally, using a spray bottle, lightly spray over the area with a solution of one part clear vinegar to four parts water. Now blot with white towels – leave a folded towel with a heavy book on top on the area overnight so that you soak up as much of the liquid as possible. You might have to repeat this a few times to flush out the rug properly, but it should neutralize any sour smell. Once the rug is dry, run the vacuum over it to restore the fluffy pile.

Q How can I remove soot spots from a light-coloured, thick-pile Chinese rug?
A Whatever you do, don't try to brush it off; you'll only spread the mark. Instead, use the vacuum cleaner nozzle attachment to suck up what you can. Then try absorbing the stain with talcum powder: sprinkle on and rub in lightly, leave a few minutes, then vacuum again. If the stain is still there, try a proprietary carpet stain remover such as 1001 Spot Shot for Carpets, from DIY stores.

Q The cheap and cheerful synthetic rugs in our holiday cottage have a glue-like attraction for dog hair. This requires considerable effort to remove, using every method previously advocated in your columns, just when we are wanting to leave. Is there any substance that could be sprayed on that would reduce the static and hasten our departure?

A Friction from the soles of your shoes is causing static build-up and attracting hairs. Synthetic fibres are hell for this. If the rugs are washable, add fabric conditioner to the final rinse and avoid over-drying – remove from the dryer while still damp, and air-dry or use anti-static tumble-dryer sheets.

Static is worse in a very dry atmosphere, so keep the cottage humid by placing bowls of water near radiators, or using pot plants in water trays; alternatively get a humidifier to increase humidity levels.

Finally, treat the rugs with an anti-static spray such as GO-Stat, available from John Lewis. Depending on traffic levels, you'll probably need to treat them every few weeks, but it should make the hairs easier to vacuum off.

Q Our natural carpet flooring is filthy. How do I clean it?
A Coir, jute and seagrass are made from plant fibres, and although they're all pretty durable, never wet-shampoo (using a 3-in-1 machine such as Vax) as over-wetting damages the fibres. Instead use a specifically formulated cleaner. Crucial Trading (01562 743747, www.crucial-trading.com) sells a Care and Cleaning Kit (£44.50 inc p&p), which includes an all-over cleaner and spot remover. They recommend you vacuum first using a suction-only cylinder cleaner – uprights with brushes can damage the fibres – before gently working the cleaner into the floor using the brush supplied. Leave to dry without walking on it, then thoroughly re-vacuum to remove the dirt. Or have it cleaned by a member of the

National Carpet Cleaners Association (0116 2719550, www.ncca.co.uk) – get quotes first.

Once you've spruced it up, treat with a soil protector to help resist stains. Intec (01794 301130, www.intecprotector.com) offers a home-use Carpet and Fabric Protector for natural flooring. It costs £62.50 inc p&p for two litres – enough for 40 sq m. They recommend applying with an air-pressurised garden sprayer using even strokes. It takes about half an hour to dry.

It's also important to vacuum regularly, except when wet and muddy (wait until dry), using a cylinder cleaner, and treat spills quickly to avoid absorption into the fibres. Again, it's important to spot-treat stains only with a specialist stain remover.

Q **What's the best way to maintain laminate flooring, and how often should it be cleaned? My cleaner is complaining it takes her longer than vacuuming carpets.**

A Laminates are pretty easy to maintain but you need to follow some rules. If it's not too busy a household, a weekly wipe-over with a barely damp mop is enough, but you mustn't wet the floor too much. For grimier floors, use a specialist laminate spray cleaner and flat microfibre mop – visit www.cleaning-laminate-flooring.com or call 0700 3450405 for a selection. Anything stronger would be too harsh, and avoid soap-based detergents such as washing-up liquid as they will leave a dull, sticky film on the floor. And don't use any product that claims to make the floor shiny or glossy: it will leave a residue and make it smeary.

To clean, spray a light mist of cleaner directly on to the dry mop-head and wipe over the floor. Dry any excess moisture immediately with a dry cloth or another mop-head; no need to rinse.

Stubborn stains can be removed with meths or acetone. Never use abrasive cleaners, including nylon scouring pads and steel wool, as they will scratch the surface. Vacuuming or sweeping two or three times a week and before you mop the floor will ensure it doesn't get too dirty and will get rid of any grit that might scratch the surface. Always use a suction-only cylinder cleaner with the hard-floor attachment – the beater bar on uprights can damage the surface (some uprights let you turn the beater bar off).

Q **We recently moved to a house with limestone tiles in the kitchen and bathroom. The kitchen ones have little potholes that are full of dirt; the bathroom tiles are also scratched. Cleaning them with a mild detergent has been unsuccessful.**

A Sounds like the surface is breaking down, hence the dirty potholes. It probably needs resealing, but first you need to deep clean. Use Lithofin Wexa (see below for details of all Lithofin products mentioned): dilute with water, as instructed, apply with a scourer and leave for 10 minutes. Scrub lightly during this time and don't let the liquid dry out. Then wipe away the dirty water and rinse with plenty of clean. Repeat if necessary, then leave for 24 hours.

Now to seal it use Lithofin MN Stain-Stop, which penetrates the stone to form an invisible film that protects the floor against spillages (except acidic stains) but still allows it to 'breathe'. Apply with a sponge, wearing rubber gloves; keep the surface wet for 10 to 20 minutes so that enough sealant has been absorbed. After 30–40 minutes, wipe off any puddles.

To stop dirt building up in the holes, apply Lithofin Multi Seal. This will fill in the holes, making the floor easier to maintain. However, it's not suitable for the bathroom as the floor could become slippery, and it doesn't allow the stone to breathe, so any water trapped underneath can't escape. But it's fine for the kitchen. Apply two or three coats with a soft brush, roller or sponge, allowing a couple of hours to dry between each one.

It sounds a faff, but once done, you won't need to reapply the Stain-Stop (just top it up every three years if you don't apply Multi Seal) and, depending on traffic, top up the Multi Seal two or three times a year. For everyday cleaning, use Lithofin Easy-Care. All products are available by mail order from Extensive (0845 2261488; www.extensive.co.uk). Your complete kit would come to £75.32 (for a 1-litre bottle of each product) including bulk-buy discounts and delivery.

Q How should I clean slate tiles and grouting on my kitchen floor? Every time I drop anything on it, a greasy mark appears, and now the grout looks grey and grubby.

A Slate is extremely durable but must be protected with a specialist sealant since, as you've discovered, it can stain. The sealing should be done when the tiles are laid, and in two stages: once before they're grouted, and again over the whole floor after they're grouted and the grout is completely dry. I imagine this was never done to your floor, or at least not on the grout joints. Here's what to do.

So that you don't seal in any dirt, first clean the tiles and grouting with a deep cleaner such as HG Super Remover (around £8.75 per litre, 01206 795200; www.hg.eu). Depending on how dirty the tiles are, this should be enough for 35–70 sq m – ample for the average-sized kitchen. Dilute one part cleaner to 10 parts water, and thoroughly scrub the tiles and grout with a brush. Rinse well.

Next you need to seal the floor. How you do this will depend on whether your tiles have been treated before. If your tiles have *never* been sealed, use HG Marble Impregnator (around £14.25 per litre) – enough for 10–20 sq m, depending on how porous your floor is. This is a one-off treatment that doesn't need regular maintenance: apply evenly over the tiles and grout in one direction with a paint roller or a non-fluffy cloth. Allow this to penetrate for up to five minutes, then remove any surplus with a dry cloth. If your tiles have been sealed, you can get away with treating just the joints using HG Super Protector for Wall and Floor Grout (around £10.65 for 250ml; enough for 30–40 sq m). For everyday cleaning, use HG Quick Porcelain Cleaner (around £5.45 per litre).

Q My terracotta floor always looks dirty, except for the areas under rugs and furniture. I want to rearrange my room – how can I sort out the dull bits?

A You need a specialist tile cleaner. Ordinary cleaners can gradually remove the protective seals from terracotta and make it more difficult to maintain. LTP Grimex (around £9.55 per litre; enough to clean 25 sq m) will remove the dirt and old superficial wax layers. Dilute one part Grimex with three parts warm water, apply, leave to react for at least five to 10 minutes, then agitate with a scourer or scrubbing brush. Rinse thoroughly with lots of clean water. Repeat if necessary. Leave to dry for at least two days – if the room is used daily, protect the floor with dustsheets.

Reseal with two coats of LTP Ironwax Satin (around £13.81 per litre; enough for 10 sq m). Pour on to the tiles, spread evenly with a soft cloth without rubbing and leave to dry for an hour before applying a second coat. You can walk on the floor after a couple of hours, but don't wet it again for three days. This allows the seal to harden and become fully resistant.

Maintain with LTP Floorshine (around £10.29 per litre; enough for 35–40 washes on a 25 sq m floor). This will clean the floor and repair the seal in areas that suffer most traffic. For stockists, or to place an order (free p&p on buys over £50; otherwise £11.50), call 01823 666213 or visit www.ltp-online.co.uk.

Q My son's Victorian flat has the original tiles on the hall floor. What's the best way to clean them to bring the colours back up?

A Sorry to say, but it's a hands-and-knees job. The dullness is down to years of dirt and layers of old wax and polish.

Use a deep cleaner, such as HG Remover, around £7.45 per litre (covers 20–50 sq m) or, for really stubborn dirt, HG Super Remover, around £8.75 per litre (covers 35–70 sq m). Dilute with water according to instructions and apply with a scrubbing brush or plastic scourer. Take care not to over-wet – you could loosen tiles. Allow to work for a few minutes, scrub well and rinse with clean water. For any hardened stains such as paint splashes, use a glass scraper held at a 45-degree angle. Never use scouring powder, wire wool or wire brushes as they'll scratch.

Once clean, finish the tiles with polish (if you can be bothered with the maintenance), but it's not essential. However, before you do you must establish whether the floor is porous (likely in the heavy-tread areas). Drip a little water on the surface. If it beads, go ahead and apply two thin coats of HG Golvpolish, around £10.95 per litre (enough for 8–10 sq m), using a paint roller or lint-free cloth. This gives a satin sheen and protects from dirt. But if the water goes in, you must seal the floor with HG Impregnator, around £13.70 per litre (enough for 8–10 sq m). This process is a one-off treatment that fills the pores and lets the polish sit on the surface but also allows any dampness in the floor to evaporate. Depending on traffic, you'll need to reapply the Golvpolish every year or so. For everyday cleaning, use HG Superfloor, around £5.19 per litre – no need to rinse. For HG products call 01206 795200 or visit www.hg.eu for stockists.

Never seal tiled floors with a resin-based or polyurethane finish; not only will it look plasticky, it might cause long-term problems by sealing in damp.

Incidentally, if there are any broken or missing tiles, Craven Dunnill Jackfield (01952 884124; www.cravendunnill-jack-field.co.uk) stocks a range of replicas, handmade to order. Prices start at £3.88 for a 6-inch square tile, plus p&p (varies on weight of order). It also offers a bespoke service but it's not cheap; the colour-matching alone costs £225 plus the price of the tiles.

Q **While waxing my legs in the kitchen, I spilt some hot wax on the laminate flooring and it stuck firmly. I have scraped off most of it, but sticky bits remain – now with dirt attached. How can I get rid of it?**

A Fill a plastic bag with ice cubes and place over the area for a few minutes. This'll harden the wax and make it easier to chip away with a plastic spatula or your fingernail. Wipe away any remaining deposits with a damp cloth and finish by washing the floor with a cleaner such as Pledge Soapy Wood Cleaner, from supermarkets.

Q We have a lovely old parquet hall floor, which hasn't been sealed. I've been using a wonderful natural wax floor polish by Wheelers of Cheshire which went on very easily and needed no buffing, rubbing or polishing. The finish always looked marvellous with very little effort. I can't find the polish any more and have been looking, without success, for an equivalent. Can you help?

A You'll be pleased to hear you can still buy the polish from Waitrose or Tesco or online at www.ecoshopdirect.co.uk (£9.99 plus £7.50 p&p for a box of five 300ml bottles, or £24.99 for a 5-litre bottle). Apply sparingly to a section of clean floor and spread with a damp cloth or mop. Repeat until all the floor is covered, then allow to dry – as you say, there's no need to buff. It's also good on quarry and slate tiles, vinyl and lino.

Our house is clean enough to be healthy,
and dirty enough to be happy

_____

Anon

Pets

Q We have a thickly woven, off-white wool rug on which our cat frequently brings up fur balls and vomit. How can I remove the unsightly stains?

A I think it's about time you treated your rug to a professional purge – that way, it'll be cleaned all over and get you back to square one. Contact the National Carpet Cleaners Association (0116 2719550, www.ncca.co.uk) for specialists in your area.

If and when your cat is sick again, act quickly. Scrape up and remove the vomit with kitchen paper or a spoon, and blot up any excess to avoid spreading the stain further. Flush with a solution of bicarbonate of soda or sponge with clear, warm water; blot dry. Now use a pet stain remover such as Bissell Pet Stain & Odour Remover (0870 2250109; www.bissell.com), or Shaws Essentials Pet Stain & Odour Eliminator (01934

831000; www.shawspet.co.uk). They contain enzymes that break down the stain, leaving the area clean and pong-free.

Q My cat has peed on the carpet. I used a carpet shampooer on wet areas, but the patches that had already dried still smell bad. Will the smell ever go?

A The odour of cat urine can be difficult to get rid of: the uric acid crystals and salts that carry the scent are insoluble and bond tightly to any surface they land on, making them resistant to regular cleaners. Any moisture that gets on the crystals reactivates them, releasing that unmistakable aroma. Matters are worsened by the fact that the uric acid changes to alkali in hours, and this can affect the carpet colour permanently if the stain isn't cleaned quickly.

One sure way to get rid of the smell is by using an enzyme-based cleaner designed for pet urine, such as Bissell OxyKIC Pet (0870 2250109 or www.bissell.com for stockists). These contain ingredients that eat the bacteria and crystals. Never use ammonia-based cleaners: there's ammonia in cat's urine, so use it and it's like calling Kitty to come and re-mark the spot.

If the pong persists, it's likely the urine has penetrated to the underlay and/or sub-floor, and there is no practical way to clean this. A new carpet might be the only solution (you may get away with replacing just the affected area) and only then if the floorboards/concrete have been scrubbed and sealed to stop the smell returning.

Q I'm at my wits' end. I have a dog and three cats and cannot keep their hairs off my clothes. Please help!

A You're always going to struggle if you don't keep your pets off the beds and sofas. If you must share your most intimate spaces with them, make your vacuum cleaner your next best friend. Invest in one that's designed to tackle pet hairs, such as the Dyson DC23 Animal (£274.03; free delivery if you buy direct from Dyson on 0800 2980298; www.dyson.co.uk; they'll even pick up and recycle your old cleaner regardless of make) and vacuum at least twice a week. This cylinder cleaner comes with a large turbine head (for carpets) and mini turbine head (ideal for stairs and upholstery) designed to lift pet hairs. Less hair on carpets and sofas means less hair on you. Also, bathe and brush your pets regularly to minimize the amount of hair and dander (dead skin flakes) they shed and to help combat odours. Always do this outside. And once you've got this licked, try these homegrown remedies. Put on a rubber glove, immerse it in water and wipe down your clothes (easier if you're wearing them), taking care not to over-wet. Rinse the glove under the tap. Alternatively, use a well-wrung-out chamois leather, dragging the cloth towards you to gather all the pet hair. If all else fails, perhaps consider getting the clippers out.

Q My German short-haired pointer moults like mad. Indoors, I can vacuum it easily, but the fur gets stuck to the carpet in the car boot. How can I get rid of the hairs (and doggy odour)?

A If your vacuum cleaner upholstery nozzle isn't up to it, put on a rubber glove, immerse it in water and rub down the carpet, taking care not to over-wet. Or use a well-wrung-out chamois, dragging the cloth towards you to gather the hair. Rinse the glove or cloth under the tap to remove the hairs.

Now for the smells. Make sure the carpet is dry, then sprinkle the boot area liberally with bicarbonate of soda. Leave for at least 15 minutes, then vacuum. Otherwise treat with 1001 No Vac Pet, from supermarkets. This quick-drying foam neutralises pet odours and there's no need to vacuum afterwards.

To stop hairs building up again, invest in a dog-friendly, protective boot liner. Over the Top Textiles (0845 6584342; www.overthetop.co.uk) make the whole caboodle, including flat mats for the boot floor and back-of-seat protectors. Prices start at £56.98 inc p&p for a standard Quiltie car mat (76 x 117cm – good for compact cars).

Pests

Q I'm so fed up – my favourite cashmere cardi has moth holes. Are there any products that deter moths but also smell nice?

A Woolly jumpers and any clothes made from natural fibres are targets for moths, especially if they are put away grubby (moths love sweat, dead skin and food remains). It's actually the larvae that do the damage, so you need to wash everything at the highest recommended temperature to kill them. For non-washable fabrics, either dry clean or put in a plastic bag and freeze for 24 hours. Temperatures below -18°C will kill the larvae. Vacuum and wipe out wardrobes and drawers with soapy water and make sure you regularly clean carpets and floors, particularly under furniture and along skirting boards.

To protect from further attacks, ensure clothes are scrupulously clean before putting away, and store woollens in anti-moth bags – John Lewis stocks lavender-scented ones. (Never use ordinary plastic bags, which attract dust and can cause condensation, leading to mildew.) Use deterrents such as Colibri The All Natural Wool Protector drawer sachets, £5 for three or £5.50 for a strip of six mini sachets, and hanging wardrobe sachets, £4.00 each (www.himalaya-uk.com; 020 8761 9250); or Total Wardrobe Care drawer sachets, £2.60 each, and hanging wardrobe sachets, £4.34 (020 7627 5609; www.totalwardrobecare.co.uk). All last up to six months, and are made from essential oils so, unlike mothballs, smell good. Alternatively, lavender, cloves, caraway seeds and cedar wood are also effective natural deterrents: again, John Lewis stocks a good range of cedar products, including Cedarwood Hang Up and Nuggets (pack of 24), both £3.90.

Finally, don't give up on your knits: send them, by special delivery, to the Cashmere Clinic (020 7584 9806), which will try to repair the holes invisibly, although they can't guarantee. Prices start at £15 per hole (they will phone you beforehand with a quote). Allow three weeks.

Q Our white PVC windows are full of fly dirt. I've tried a few products but the unsightly spots remain. Any ideas?
A You need Nilco uPVC Cleaner (NB: the correct name for PVC is PVCu but it's also know as uPVC, just to confuse things) from Lakeland (01539 488100; www.lakeland.co.uk). It'll remove dirt on weather-worn uPVC doors, window frames and garden furniture. Apply with a clean cloth and rub

over the surface; no need to rinse. At other times wash the frames with hot soapy water.

Q **A cream-coloured lampshade made of stretched fabric has several fly spots on it which have baked hard on to the surface. What's the best way to get rid?**

A Dabbing the spots with a weak solution of washing-up liquid sometimes works, but there's always the chance that you could end up with lighter patches, or watermarks (especially on silk shades), or removing the surface finish. Your best plan is to treat the whole shade, in the bath, using warm water and a little biological washing powder. Soap the surface of the shade and very gently work the solution over the stains from both sides, using an old soft-bristled toothbrush. Rinse well, attach a length of string to the holder and drip-dry over the bath to prevent any ring marks. Finish off with a hairdryer. If any trim should come unstuck, use a little adhesive to re-attach.

Q **How can I get rid of ants? I live in a ground-floor flat and every summer they come through the living-room floorboards. I put down insecticide powder, which helps, but each year they reappear. What can I do to stop them coming back?**

A Ants start appearing from April, are prolific in July and August and slacken off in October. They're harmless but, let's face it, they're not invited. Track down the source and, if you can, pour a kettle of boiling water over it. If you can't find where they're coming in, use Nippon Ant Bait Station (comes with two traps), from hardware stores and garden centres. It contains an insecticide that the ants eat and regurgitate back at the nest, which then kills the colony. Place where you see them coming into the house – you can use inside or out and it works for up to three months, depending on the weather and size of nest (you may need more than one trap). The problem may worsen before it improves as the traps are designed to attract the beasties.

If you're against the idea of killing, a sprinkle of cayenne pepper, scented talc or peppermint oil placed along the skirting boards should put them off. If you try everything to no avail, contact your local authority pest control department (you'll probably have to pay). Or contact the British Pest Control Association (01332 294288; www.bpca.org.uk or www.pestaware.org.uk). Don't leave out food scraps, and keep fruit and veg in the fridge.

Q **Help! My sitting room is a woodlice cemetery. They climb through an airbrick and down a skirting board, only to die on the carpet, to which they stick. How can I stop this? I vacuum regularly, but the hordes keep coming.**

A Woodlice are crustaceans that live on rotten wood and vegetable matter in cool, damp areas, occasionally venturing from their homes – under stones, clumps of plants, logs or doormats – into yours, between September and April. They're usually searching for shelter, and although they're capable of chewing damage to plant leaves, they're completely harmless. However, they do indicate the presence of damp. In centrally heated houses, they quickly dry out and die, hence the pile of bodies in the morning. If they're a nuisance, tackle the dampness and remove anything that might be causing it – for example plants, leaf litter or stacks of logs – from the outside walls. Then seal off potential entry points and fill in gaps between skirting boards and paving stones. Take care not to block air vents, though (overgrown or blocked vents should be cleared). You can cover them with fine mesh from hardware stores (this allows air to circulate, but keeps pests out) but never put mesh over vents for gas appliances. Replace loose or decaying mortar. In extreme cases, use an insecticide powder or long-lasting spray suitable for crawling insects around entry points into the house.

Q In my carpets, curtains and books I have an infestation of what I am told are 'woolly bears' – small, grub-like creatures. How can I get rid of them and prevent them returning?

A These are carpet beetle grubs. The adults are 2–4mm long, look like mottled brown, grey and cream ladybirds, and they thrive in centrally heated homes. Stuart Hine, who manages the Insect Information Service at the Natural History Museum in London, tells me they are extremely common – and that I probably have them in my own home (surely not!).

The larvae are about the same length as the adults and look like maggots with brown hairs (hence the name woolly bears). If you spot them, act quickly as they'll be looking for fabrics in which to lay their eggs. As the larvae hatch, they munch through their surroundings, leaving holes similar to those made by clothes moths.

It's important to trace the source. Birds' nests, animal remains or dead insects are favourite hang-outs, so search the loft first for signs. Then look for traces of damage in airing cupboards, wardrobes and chests where clothes and blankets are stored, as well as under carpets and rugs.

Clean up if you spot signs: launder or dry clean affected items, vacuum carpets thoroughly (then empty the bag straight away). For minor infestations, spray floorboards and corners of cupboards with an insecticide suitable for crawling insects, such as Rentokil Insectrol Dust for Carpet Beetle, from hardware stores (or call 0151 5485050 for stockists). Otherwise, call in the experts: to find a local specialist, contact the British Pest Control Association (01332 294288; www.bpca. org.uk or www.pestaware.org.uk).

To prevent a recurrence, make sure you clean thoroughly, taking care to remove fluff, particularly under and behind furniture, and vacuum carpets thoroughly.

Q **We are plagued with tiny black mites in the kitchen cupboards. They live in the wood behind the shelves and feed on cereal. We clean the cupboards often and have**

tried insecticide, but they always come back. Any suggestions?

A The lovely people at the British Pest Control Association (BPCA) say it's very difficult to identify them without seeing them. So here's an invitation: catch some and send to the Insect Identification Department, British Pest Control Association, Gleneagles House, 1 Vernongate, South Street, Derby DE1 1UP. The easiest way to do this is to carefully press sticky tape on to the mites, then fold this over and put it in an empty matchbox. The insect inspectors will identify and tell you where they come from, what they eat, whether they're harmful and how to get rid. The service usually takes up to two weeks and is free. The BPCA will also give you details of pest controllers in your area; contact 01332 294288 or visit their websites at www.bpca.org.uk or www.pestaware.org.uk.

Q My son is asthmatic and while I can wash bed linen at 60 degrees, duvets are more difficult. Is there a washing powder I can buy to counter mites? Also, are anti-allergy pillow covers effective?

A Dust mite excrement is one of the main triggers for asthma, causing allergic reactions in 85 per cent of asthmatic children. You're right in saying that washing at 60 degrees or above kills mites, but when this isn't practical, use Anti-Allergy Laundry Detergent (£22.61 inc p&p for a litre), available from Allergymatters (020 8339 0029; www.allergymatters.com. Although much more expensive than ordinary detergent, it's good for all fabrics including delicate items that can't be washed at 60°C, and you can use it in the machine or by hand. It neutralises the dust mite allergens (and also works on pet dander, mildew, mould and smoke), so they can't cause an allergic reaction. One bottle is enough for about 32 loads.

The pillow covers are also a good idea, but for full protection, get a cover for the duvet and mattress as well. Mattress covers should enclose the whole mattress, not just the top and sides like a fitted sheet. However, you need to take other measures too, such as replacing carpets with hard flooring, regularly vacuuming and damp dusting (hard work, I know). Allergy UK (01322 619898; www.allergyuk.org) can give you more information as well as advice on the best type of anti-allergy bedding for you.

Q My son is coming home after a gap year abroad. He's not the most hygienic and has been living pretty roughly so I'm concerned that he might return with, for example, bed bugs in his luggage – I've heard they're on the increase. What precautions do I need to take?

A Well, I like to be optimistic, but it's true that bed bugs are on the rise. They thrive in dirty places (infested rooms may have bugs under wallpaper or in joinery cracks) and can easily be transported in luggage, so perhaps you should be cautious.

The adult bug resembles a small brown disc, about the size of a match head.

Although not disease-carriers, they emerge to feed at night (blood from their adult hosts!) and their bite can cause severe irritation. They also give off an unpleasant smell. Tell-tale signs are: blood spotting and brown excrement spots on bedding; opaque eggs. They are really difficult to eradicate and if you think you have them, you will need professional help. Contact the British Pest Control Association (01332 294288; www.bpca.org.uk) for experts in your area.

Q I've discovered silverfish in my (otherwise clean) kitchen. I've scrubbed it from top to bottom and think I'm rid of them all. How can I make sure the horrors stay away?

A Silverfish give me the creeps too, and it's probably little comfort to you to know they are harmless. They love moisture and often lurk inside plugholes, feeding off starchy food scraps. They also love damp books and are partial to wallpaper paste. They forage at night in damp areas, where they can live for more than three years, laying their eggs in cracks. During the day, they hide behind wallpaper, skirting boards and beneath loose floor coverings.

Your answer is to sort damp spots or condensation. Check sinks and behind the washing machine and dishwasher for leaks, and make sure there aren't any crevices that can harbour damp or provide hidey-holes. You can buy specific insecticides, but they're not ideal in an area where food is being prepared.

Q How can I stop flies crawling behind the roof blinds in my conservatory? Every autumn I have to pay someone to clean them and dispose of all the dead bodies.

A First, starve them – don't leave any food scraps out, and keep all fruit and veg in the fridge. Always cover defrosting food. Your kitchen bin needs a tight-fitting lid – flies love to lay eggs in rubbish (up to 150 at a time). Keep bins away from windows and doors, especially if you use one for organic waste. Fit door and window fly screens (you get the ventilation but keep the flies out). Pest Control Direct (01323 846845; www.pestcontroldirect.co.uk) does a selection, including hinge screens for windows. Prices start at £55.35 (inc p&p) for a window 650 x 950mm. Use a glue board fly-killer. A UV light attracts the flies, but unlike the commercial units, it uses sticky paper instead of an electric grid, and is less garish. For example, the Flypod (£56.81; replacement glue boards £12.77 for six – all inc p&p) from Group 55 Ltd (01772 310200; www.pestcontrolshop.co.uk). Coverage is about 30 sq m. Finally, grow strongly scented flowers, such as marigolds and pelargoniums near doors or on windowsills.

Q I have recently seen evidence of mice – droppings – in our flat. My partner isn't nearly as bothered as I am. How can I convince him that we need to get rid of them?

A Try telling him this: as well as carrying diseases, mice can do a lot of damage – they can chew through electric cables, water and gas pipes and woodwork. The average mouse deposits 70 droppings in 24 hours and is incontinent (just imagine them

scurrying over your kitchen worktops and weeing freely).
Warfarin was commonly used to kill mice but now most are
immune to it. And forget about traps – they don't seem to
catch that many (and nor do mice like cheese). A rodenticide
is what's needed, plus mouse-proofing as far as possible: stuff
any small holes with wire wool sprinkled with peppermint oil.

If the problem gets really bad, find a pest control expert in
your Yellow Pages or call your local authority, who will probably make a charge, but I reckon it's more than worth it.

**Q I have what I think are moths in my flour and have
thrown it away. They give me the creeps – how do I stop
them returning?**
A Flour moths are pale in colour and their larvae feed on
stored foods such as grain, cereals, dried fruit, flour and nuts
– they can even chew their way through cardboard boxes and
polythene bags. Buy dry foodstuffs in small quantities and
keep them in well-sealed plastic or glass containers. Flour and
the like stored for over six months is often the source of infestation, so routinely check containers. Freeze nuts and use
directly from the freezer.

If you notice an infestation, throw away the contents of the
container and wash it well. Examine unopened food packages
thoroughly and if you have the slightest suspicion, throw it
out. Vacuum into the corners (moths like to lay their eggs
there) and clean up any spills and crumbs. Wash shelves with
very hot soapy water and dry well before replacing foodstuffs.
And empty the vacuum cleaner before any eggs hatch!

Dirt is not dirt, but only
something in the wrong place.

3rd Viscount Palmerston, Henry John Temple

Freshening things up

Q You often recommend bicarbonate of soda as a cleaning and freshening agent, but I can't find quantities larger than the diddy tubs on the home-baking shelves. Where can I bulk-buy it?

A I'm a big fan and get through loads of the stuff. My homemade scouring mix is a winner: add it to bleach to form a paste – great for removing soap scum from shower tiles when rubbed on with a nylon pad. Here are a few companies selling in bulk: Just A Soap (01284 735043; www.justasoap.co.uk; minimum order £10) – available in 5kg (£4.82) and above; and The Soap Kitchen (01805 622944; www.thesoap-kitchen.co.uk) – available from 500g (£1.15). Postage charges depend on order size. Bicarb is cheap but the p&p rates whack up the price, so better to order in bulk – it keeps for yonks.

★ TOP TIP ★
Getting the musty smell out of old books...

Bicarbonate of soda usually works. Place your book open inside a freezer bag (use separate bags for each book) and add four tablespoons of bicarb. Seal and leave for two to three weeks. When you remove the book from the bag, the bicarb will have absorbed the musty smell without harming the book. Better still, the bicarb can then be recycled: just pour it down the sink and follow it with a kettle of boiling water to freshen up your plughole.

Q My teenage son has the smelliest trainers imaginable. I have endlessly bought those inserts that are supposed to absorb the odour, but they're not cutting it. Any other ideas?

A It's a difficult one, especially in hot weather, but here's something that might help. Sprinkle a fine layer of bicarbonate of soda in the shoes at night; this will help to neutralise the smell. Empty out in the morning, then replace with a few drops of tea tree oil, which is anti-bacterial and a great masker of bad odours. Machine-wash at least once a week at 40°C with a biological detergent on a slow spin and allow to air-dry.

Q When I took my gold jewellery out of the safe, some of the pieces were tarnished. How do I get them shiny again?

A The purer the gold, the less it tarnishes – it's the other metals mixed in that discolour. And if you haven't worn your jewellery for a couple of years, the tarnish has had a chance to build up. When you wear jewellery, it is constantly rubbing against your clothes and other surfaces, which keeps the tarnish at bay.

To get everything sparkling again, soak in lemon juice or use a proprietary gold cleaner such as Town Talk Jewel Sparkle for Gold & Diamonds (£5.28 for 225ml inc p&p; 01204 520014). This comes with a little basket that you immerse in the liquid, so it's ideal for rings and earrings. For larger pieces use either Town Talk Gold Polishing Cloth (£4.46 inc p&p – 30 x 45cm) or Silvo Liquid, from supermarkets.

If you're putting them away again, wrap in a bag impregnated with anti-tarnish agents. Town Talk sells various sizes from £7.59 inc p&p for a 15 x 15cm bag.

Q **I have a rose pendant carved from ivory, which belonged to my grandmother. She died in 1946 and I don't think it's been worn since. How do I clean the intricate carving without damaging it?**
A Use tepid water to which you've added a drop of washing-up liquid. Don't immerse the pendant for too long – ivory is porous and can absorb moisture, which will cause it to stain. With a baby's toothbrush, gently remove the trapped dirt, then rinse and dry immediately with a soft cloth. To keep in good condition, dust with a soft cloth and occasionally apply

a light film of almond oil. If you have no success, or if the pendant is valuable, consult an expert at the British Antique Dealers' Association (020 7589 4128; www.bada.org). Finally, always apply your make-up, perfume and hairspray before putting on the pendant, otherwise it can stain the ivory. And make sure you store it away from direct heat and strong sunlight, which will bleach it.

Q What's the best way of cleaning a small chandelier without the faff of taking it down?

A The best (if not the easiest) way is to get up on a ladder and remove the glass droplets one by one and wash them in a warm mild solution of washing-up liquid. Rinse and pat dry with a lint-free cloth. Work in sections so you know where you are, and wipe the arms and centrepiece with a damp cloth before replacing the droplets. (Sounds obvious, but don't forget to turn off the electricity before you start.) Unless you have smokers in the house or run a coal fire, you shouldn't need to clean it again for at least a year.

If this sounds too long-winded, use a spray such as Antiquax Chandelier & Crystal Cleaner (0870 9089327; www.antiquax.info). Although not as effective as doing it by hand, it's certainly easier and quicker. You spray the chandelier (avoiding any electric bits) until the cleaner and dirt drip off on to newspaper placed below. Once the dirt's dealt with, allow any remaining cleaner to dry, and you should be left with a streak-free sparkling finish.

And if your chandelier ever needs a repair, contact Wilkinson Plc (020 8314 1080; www.wilkinson-plc.com). They stock thousands of parts and can recreate any missing droplets or make replacement arms.

Q **I'm having difficulty cleaning the inside of a decanter that has acquired a white encrustation. Even sterilisation tablets won't shift it.**

A Fill the decanter with vinegar up to the encrustation, add a handful of dry rice and swirl it around to loosen the deposits; leave overnight. Wash and rinse with hot clean water. Leave to drain upside down, and replace the stopper only when completely dry.

If that doesn't work, try a limescale remover for descaling plastic kettles – wear rubber gloves and apply it neat, rubbing gently with an old toothbrush or bottlebrush. Rinse immediately.

Still no joy? Then the hard-water deposits will have attacked the glass, in which case you'll need to have it professionally cleaned. Some companies who do this are: Blue Crystal Glass (020 7278 0142; www.bluecrystalglass.co.uk), who charge around £34.50 per decanter. Service takes about three to four weeks.

Redhouse Glass Crafts (01384 399460). They charge from £14 per decanter. Service takes up to four weeks depending on the cleaning method used. Wilkinson Plc (020 8314 1080; www.wilkinson-plc.com); they charge around £52 per decanter. Service takes eight to 10 weeks.

All these companies say you should either post the decanter by special delivery (wrap it up well!) or deliver it personally. If the decanter is very valuable, Wilkinson Plc can arrange a courier for an extra charge.

Q I love fresh flowers and display them in clear glass vases, but I can't remove the bloom from the glass. Any tips?

A This is the result of hard-water deposits, which in turn causes grime to cling. Crystal vases, particularly older ones and those with a high lead content, are the worst offenders as the glass is porous and dirt gets trapped in it, making it harder to clean. Try filling the vase with vinegar and a handful of dry rice. Swirl around to loosen the deposits, leave overnight, then rinse with hot, soapy water and drain upside down. Alternatively, try a limescale remover for plastic kettles – wear rubber gloves and apply neat, rubbing gently with an old toothbrush. Rinse immediately.

To help keep vases clean, always use a flower food (most bought flowers come with a sachet). It helps prolong the life of the flowers and reduces the amount of waste polluting the water. Chrysal Clear Cut Flower Food (attached to most large supermarket flowers) helps reduce the build-up of hard-water deposits. Finally, top up the water regularly to reduce crusty deposits forming as water levels reduce; roses and tulips are notoriously thirsty. And clean the vases as soon as they're emptied. For more flower care tips, visit www.flowers.org.uk.

Q We've moved to a house with a stained-glass porch where the lead is filthy. How can I brighten it up?

A There are two distinct types of stained glass: coloured and painted. Each needs to be treated differently and never with a proprietary window cleaner.

Coloured glass (known as decorative leaded lights) is made by adding chemicals during the manufacture. You can tell it's this type if the design is created solely with lead. With a flower, for example, the lead would be used to form the shape of the petals. If this is what you have, clean inside and out with a very mild, warm soapy solution and a soft cloth. Don't rub hard, especially near the edges, in case you disturb the cement between glass and the lead, and don't over-wet or allow water to run down. Gently buff dry with a soft, lint-free cloth.

Painted glass, known as stained glass, is where vitreous enamels are painted on to clear or coloured glass (usually on the inside) to create a design. It's then kiln-fired to fuse the paint to the glass. If you have this type, clean only the outside (as above), and then only if you're sure there's no paint there. For the inside (or if you're unsure), you should call in a specialist, or you risk removing the paint. Contact the Conservation Register (020 7785 3804; www.conservationregister.com) or the Building Conservation Directory (01747 871717; www.buildingconservation.com) for specialists who will be able to advise you on cleaning and repairs.

I can recommend *The National Trust Manual of Housekeeping*, a comprehensive guide to caring for fragile fittings and fixtures (there's a whole chapter on cleaning windows). Order at www.elsevierdirect.com/conservation or phone 01865 474010.

Q The insides of my pewter goblets have become badly discoloured. How do I get them looking great again?
A It depends on how old the goblets are. Pre-18th-century pewter is made from lead and tin, and it's the lead that causes the pewter to turn black and tarnish. Unfortunately, there's nothing you can do to remove this.

Modern pewter is made almost entirely of tin, is shinier and looks like silver. It's a soft metal, so don't use an abrasive cleaner or clean it more than once a year.

If your goblets are modern, there are two ways you can clean them, depending on whether you want a shiny look or a more traditional dull grey. To make them sparkle, you'll need to use a polish, such as Maas Metal Polishing Crème from Lakeland (01539 488100; www.lakeland.co.uk). It's highly concentrated and can also be used on stainless steel, silver, gold, brass and chrome. If you prefer a more traditional finish, wipe with cotton wool dipped in meths, then wash in warm soapy water and dry well with a soft cloth.

As your goblets are so tarnished, you might have to try the first method initially, but after that, you should be able to get away with the second, if you prefer the dull look.

Q My cast-iron grate and surround are covered in splashes and smears. I was recommended Zebo but it only seemed to highlight the marks. I have tried re-polishing but now it's all dark swirls and splodges. What can I do?

A It sounds as if you're either applying too much polish and/or using too soft a cloth when buffing. Your best option is to remove the old layers of polish with a rag soaked in white spirit and start again. Then you can re-blacken the grate and surround with either (as Zebo is now discontinued) Liberon Iron Paste (01797 367555) or Hotspot Black Stove and Grate Polish (01403 787700; www.hotspotonline.co.uk).

The secret is to apply the paste *very* sparingly using a brush or cloth and work in small sections at a time. Build up the polish in thin layers, allowing it to dry for a few minutes between coats, and then buff to a shine with a brush or old towel. Don't use a soft cloth as it won't have enough oomph for levelling out the polish to give a good shine without smears.

If all that sounds too much like hard work, use a heat-resistant paint such as Woodstove by Plasti-kote (01223 836400; www.plasti-kote.com), Hammerite High Heat Paint (0870 4441111; www.hammerite.co.uk) or Hotspot High Temperature Stove Paint (01403 787700, www.hotspotonline.co.uk) to give a long-term finish. All are available in aerosol form from DIY stores.

Q I have a wood-burning stove, but within 30 minutes of lighting the fire, the glass is so thick with soot I can't see any flames! How can I keep it clear while the fire is burning?

A You're either not burning the right type of fuel or your stove is old and not working efficiently. Ensure you use dry, well-seasoned wood that's been stored under cover for at least a year and brought inside a week before burning. And if you ever use coal, ensure it's smokeless. It's also good to run the stove with plenty of flames for half an hour after each fuelling and before shutting down for a period of slow burning.

If your stove is over 20 years old, it's unlikely to have an 'air wash' or 'clean burn' system. A wash of very hot air ensures the fuel burns completely and keeps the glass clean if operated correctly (most new models have this). So if yours isn't clean-burning, soot build-up will always be a problem. However, you can lessen the effects by always burning decent fuel, having the flue swept twice a year, and closing the air inlet once the fire is burning well.

To clean the glass the next morning, the easiest – and cheapest – way is to rub it with a piece of damp newspaper or kitchen towel dipped in the wood ash. For particularly stubborn marks, use a nylon scouring pad.

Q We've just moved into our house and the hearth of the stone fireplace has soot marks – how do we get rid of them?

A Depending on the type of stone, these can be hard to remove, particularly if they've been absorbed deep into the surface. And without knowing which stone your fireplace is made from, I'd say your best plan is to use a generic stone cleaner such as Lithofin Wexa, £17.75 per litre inc p&p – enough to treat 5–25 sq m. Buy it from Extensive (0845 2261488; www.extensive.co.uk). Although this may not be as effective as a specialised treatment for a specific stone, it's safe to use on all types.

Just dilute with water, as instructed on the can, apply with a scourer and leave to work for 10 minutes. Scrub the surface lightly during this time and don't let the product dry out. Then wipe away the dirty water and rinse with plenty of clean water. Repeat if you need to. And if you can identify the type of stone, you should contact Extensive for further advice.

Q My home's previous owners used to burn candles on the mantelpiece, which have left wax marks splattered up the wall. I've chipped it off with my fingernails but the stains remain. What now?
A You need International Stain Block Paint, from DIY stores, which you apply with a natural bristle brush or roller suitable for solvent-based paint. It's also available in aerosol form with an upward spraying nozzle for the tops of walls or ceilings. You can add an overcoat of ordinary emulsion about four hours later.

Q I used the Velcro system to hang some pre-gathered net curtains, but now the backing on the PVC window is no longer sticky. How can I remove the old glue, as the curtains are constantly sagging?

A Without knowing the type of glue, it's difficult to give a specific answer. But the good people at Everest, the window company, have some tips.

Try removing the glue with white spirit and a soft cloth. If that doesn't work, use a hard plastic spatula, but be careful not to scratch the uPVC. It should now be possible to get rid of any remainder with a PVC cream cleaner such as Nilco uPVC Cleaner from Lakeland (01539 488100; www.lakeland.co.uk), finishing off with a soft cloth.

If it's still not budging, get in touch with the window supplier – some offer a polishing service. Otherwise look up 'double glazing repair' in the *Yellow Pages*.

Q We want to replace our net curtains, which need frequent washing, with the film that can be applied to windows to give the same effect. Can you help?

A I can recommend Brume window film (01364 73951; www.brume.co.uk) – everyone in my road has the fanlight (glass above the front door) done in this type of film, with the street number cut out. Brume does either plain film with the effect of sandblasted glass or one with integral cutout patterns. It's fairly easy to apply, as long as you follow the instructions to the letter. (Brume will happily send you a sample to try out.) Prices depend on size and design, but as a guide, an 80 x 120cm piece will set you back £60 inc p&p.

Q Our 10-year-old stainless-steel cutlery set we use every day – and put in the dishwasher – is perfect apart from the bowls of the spoons, which have turned dark grey. How can I get their sparkle back?

A Although stainless steel is tough and relatively stain-free, it still needs a bit of care. The staining is probably caused by food left on the cutlery while waiting to be washed. Put a teaspoon of biological washing powder into a mug of hot water and soak the spoons overnight. If that doesn't do it, try De-Solv-It Crockery De-Stainer (safe to use on cutlery, although not on aluminium or silver-plate) – www.desolvit.co.uk. Dissolve six capfuls in 1 litre of hot water, soak the spoons for four to five hours or leave overnight, then rinse thoroughly and wash in warm soapy water before use. To stop it happening again, rinse cutlery before loading the dishwasher and never use the rinse-and-hold cycle as the humid atmosphere can cause staining.

Q We have a well-used dinner service we refer to as The Everyday Set. It's in perfect condition except that the plates are marked by stainless-steel cutlery. Over the years these grey, pencil-type marks have built up to the extent that they now make an otherwise perfect dinner set look tatty. No amount of washing or scrubbing removes the marks. Can you help?

A The marks are caused by tiny deposits of metal from the cutlery and, as you say, don't come off easily. You need to use a mild abrasive such as salt, bicarbonate of soda, cream metal polish, toothpaste or denture powder. Rub it on the affected area with a damp cloth, wash off and, hey presto, your china will sparkle anew. For stubborn marks, use Bar Keepers Friend, available from supermarkets.

Q I polish my household silver with my huge stash of creams and cloths, but for jewellery I prefer to use a 'silver bath'. This seems to have disappeared off the face of the earth – help!

A You're probably talking about Goddard's Silver Dip, which is still available from hardware stores. Dips are great for small, fiddly items such as jewellery, converting the tarnish (silver sulphide) back into silver, removing the sulphide and leaving the silver behind – though don't use on pearls, corals or opals.

Make your own dip by lining a plastic bowl with aluminium foil. Fill with very hot water and add a handful of washing soda. Immerse your silver, ensuring it's in contact with the foil. An electrochemical reaction removes the silver sulphide and deposits it on the foil.

For large items that come above the water line, turn over after five minutes. When the foil darkens, replace. Immerse items for up to 10 minutes only. Whichever dip you use, always follow manufacturer's time limits. Don't use on heavily tarnished items as you could be left with a dull white finish.

Avoid getting dip on stainless-steel knife blades – it can stain. And don't use on damaged silver-plate that's patchy, as it can attack the base metal.

Q **Where can I get my silver cutlery re-plated? And how much should I expect to pay? Also, is there any harm in using the cutlery when it's worn down to the base metal?**
A Try looking in the *Yellow Pages* or on the internet for 'electroplaters' and you'll come across dozens of companies. As long as your cutlery is decent stuff, re-plating is usually worth it, although it may not have the same just-new surface shine: expect to pay around £5 for a teaspoon and £6 for a dessert-spoon or a soup spoon, depending on the thickness. This works out at roughly a third of the price of new. The process involves stripping off the old silver plate to expose the base metal, before buffing and re-polishing to remove minor dents and scratches. The cutlery is then re-plated to the thickness you want – in theory one micron equates to roughly one year's daily use. So 25 microns should last 25 years. When posting your cutlery, send it registered. Finally, unless the silver plate is actually peeling, you won't come to any harm if you carry on using the cutlery, even if the plate has worn down to the base metal.

Q **I've inherited a lot of brassware from my mother, but can't stand the smell of brass cleaner. Is there an alternative?**

A Lemon juice and salt works well on brass. Either mix to a paste (one part lemon juice to three parts salt) or rub surfaces with half a lemon dipped in salt. The lemon cuts through the grease, and the salt acts as a mild abrasive. But don't leave on too long as it could pit the surface. Rinse and buff dry with a soft cloth. You could also use tomato ketchup, Worcestershire sauce or non-gel toothpaste. Again, rinse immediately after cleaning and buff dry.

Q Is it possible to remove a blood stain from a mattress?
A The sooner you get to it, the bigger the chance of success. Tip the mattress on its side and, holding a towel beneath the stained area to avoid spreading the mark, sponge with cold water. Blot thoroughly with kitchen paper and keep wetting and blotting until no more colour transfers on to the paper. Treat with a foam carpet or upholstery shampoo, then rinse and blot dry. The mattress cover may well take on a ring mark but I guess that's preferable to what you have now.

Q Last winter I stored a brand-new sateen mattress upright, in its plastic, against the back wall of a spare room in our old cottage, without realising that condensation was building up between the cold wall and mattress. Now one side of the mattress is dotted with mould. How can I get rid of it?
A Prop the mattress on its side – to avoid over-wetting – and dab the marks with a solution of water and Milton Sterilising

Fluid, from supermarkets. But be prepared to be persistent; the older the mildew, the harder it is to shift. Start with a dilute solution and get more concentrated until the spots are cleared. Rinse immediately by sponging with cold water, then blot dry.

Q **Whatever happened to that wonderful dry-cleaning spray called K2r? I can't find it anywhere any more. It was superb at instantly removing grease spots on clothes.**
A It is indeed excellent, and you'll be pleased to hear you can still buy it from Robert Dyas (call 0845 4503004 to find your nearest store, or order online at www.robertdyas.co.uk). They sell the K2r Stain Remover Spray for £2.99 for 100ml.

Q **I spend a fortune sending work clothes to the dry cleaner. What happened to those dry-cleaning sheets that went in the tumble-dryer? I can't find them in the shops any more.**
A Lakeland (01539 488100; www.lakeland.co.uk) sells a dry cleaning kit by Hagerty (£8.80). It comes with a reusable, dryer-safe bag and four impregnated sheets to clean up to 16 garments. Pre-treat stains with the sheet, then place your clothes in the bag along with the sheet, and put in the dryer on a low or delicate heat for 20 minutes.

The heat from the dryer activates ingredients on the sheet, releasing vapours that are supposed to clean and freshen. Neat idea, but as the sheets contain none of the powerful chemicals used by professional dry cleaners, they can't handle large or deep-set stains, and are good only for freshening up.

Q Where can I get fuller's earth powder? I find it better than talc for taking grease marks out of suede and it's certainly cheaper than dry cleaning. But the chemist doesn't stock it any more.

A Fuller's earth is made from clay and is certainly an excellent de-greaser for removing oil, grease and fat spills from all sorts of things including silk, wool, suede, furniture, carpets, wooden and stone floors. It's even used in cosmetics (makes a great face-pack), cat litter and to absorb agents used in chemical warfare. I've tracked down a supplier called Fishing With Style (0113 2507244; www.fishingwithstyle.co.uk). Strange name, I know, but fuller's earth is also used in fly-fishing (it de-greases the line and helps it sink!). The company sells it by mail order, either in a 100 g resealable tub for £3.90 or 1 kg bag for £12.75 (all prices inc p&p).

Q The 2.2m-high windows of my Paris studio flat have white, narrow-slatted blinds that have become grey with accumulated dust. What's the best way to clean them? (There's no bath to soak them in – only a small shower cubicle.)

A It's a boring, fiddly job at the best of times, but here's something that will lessen the pain. It's called the Microfibre Venetian Blind Duster from Lakeland (01539 488100;

www.lakeland.co.uk). This specially designed tool allows you to clean three slats at a time with just one wipe. It can be used dry to dust or wet to clean (use plain water – no need for cleaning sprays or polishes) and comes with a replacement machine-washable microfibre sleeve.

Q Although my windows are double-glazed, mould has grown on the lining of the curtains. I had them dry cleaned but the mould hasn't gone. The dry cleaner says there is nothing he can do as it's a living organism. What now, please?

A The dry cleaner is right: mildew is a fungus that feeds on fibres and dry cleaning won't shift the marks. The fact that you can't wash your curtains means you're limited as to what action you can take. Fresh spores can sometimes be wiped away, but the older the mildew, the harder it is to remove.

Try bleaching the marks with a solution of Milton Sterilising Fluid, from supermarkets. Take care not to get it on the curtain fabric (separate the linings without unstitching by lifting them up from the bottom). For extra security, place a folded towel between curtain and lining. Test first, then if you're happy, start with a dilute solution and get more concentrated until the spots go. Rinse immediately by sponging with cold water, and blot dry. If this doesn't work, you'll need to have the curtains re-lined.

Q I recently bought a 1960s umbrella in superb condition, except the fabric's a bit dirty (polyester/cotton, and it's lost some water repellency). How can I clean it and improve the water repellency?

A If sponging with warm water doesn't clean it, you'll need something stronger, but not washing-up liquid, because it contains salts that'll strip what's left of the proofing. Instead, use a soap-based cleaner such as Nikwax Tech Wash, around £4.49 for 300ml (for stockists call 01892 786400 or visit www.nikwax.com). Erect the brolly outside, dilute the cleaner in warm water and work up a lather with a sponge, using long, sweeping strokes. While still wet, finish with a waterproofer such as Nikwax Cotton Proof, around £6.99 for 300ml (stockists as above). Don't use shoe re-proofer because you'll get patchy results. Leave to air-dry.

If this all sounds like too much work, or if the stains aren't shifting, contact Fox Umbrellas Ltd (020 8662 0022; www.foxumbrellas.com) who make and restore umbrellas. They can re-cover it for around £40.

Q My pale tan suede Timberland boots have a mayonnaise stain. I normally use baby shampoo on them, but it's not helping. What's the answer?

A You may not be able to remove the grease completely, but you can make it less noticeable by spreading it. Apply a few drops of 40/60-grade petroleum spirit, available from chemists, to the stain and leave overnight. Use a soft toothbrush to brush the edges of the mark gently between applications – it'll take a few goes. If the stain persists, try dyeing, but don't do this before tackling the grease, as the marked area may darken or not take on the dye.

Q My workplace is introducing hot-desking. While I don't mind my own germs I'm not happy sharing everyone else's. Is there a disinfectant for keyboard, mouse and phone?

A I don't blame you one bit. The average desk habours more disease-causing bacteria than a toilet seat, which is a scary thought. And given that some cold and flu bugs can survive on surfaces for up to 72 hours, you have every right to be concerned.

IXOS XC17-A Antibacterial Wet & Dry Wipes (contact 01844 219000; www.ixos.co.uk for stockists) are safe to use on all plastic (except LCD and TFT screens) and metal surfaces, and claim to reduce bacteria levels by 99.9 per cent if surfaces are treated daily. Clean equipment with a wet wipe and run over with a dry one.

Q I have lots of shoes in different colours, therefore lots of pots of polish. Long before the tins are finished, the contents become dry and unusable. How can I revive them?

A Oh, I like your frugality. Add a dash of white spirit to the tin – use your judgment, depending on how much polish is left –

then replace the lid and leave in a warmish place, such as the airing cupboard (not near a naked flame), until the polish has absorbed the white spirit and softened.

Q Where can I buy a set of top-quality shoe-brushes? I use the ones my father had in the war: great quality, but starting to show their age. I would like to replace them with equally sturdy brushes.

A I also use my dad's wartime brushes, which, now you mention it, are getting a little short in the bristle. But have a look at those made by Shoe-String. The Luxury Polish Dauber (£2.50) is pure horsehair with a rounded tip to fit inside cream polish jars. For buffing, there's the Luxury Shoe Brush (£4.80), also horsehair. Alternatively, buy a Shoe Brush Two-Pack (£4.00), incorporating a pair of rectangular pure-bristle brushes. All have wooden handles. For stockists, call 01858 467467, or you can order direct from www.shoestringuk.com (add p&p which varies on the value of your order).

Q I have eczema – what's the best way to clean my make-up brushes and keep them free of bacteria?

A This may sound obvious, but your facial cleanser is probably the best thing as you know it won't cause a reaction. If your skin is sensitive, one to try might be Lavera Neutral Cleansing Gel from Allergy Matters (020 8339 0029; www.allergy matters.com). It removes make-up and is fragrance free. Squeeze a little into a basin of warm water, swish the brushes around until clean, then rinse under the tap with plenty of warm water. Pat with a towel and allow to dry naturally.

Q **My daughter owns a very large and solid toy sheep – one you can sit on – and he's become rather grubby. His fur looks like sheep's wool, but I'm not sure what the material actually is. What can I do to freshen him up?**

A Just sponge him down gently with a little warm water and a drop of mild detergent for washing woollens, followed by a clean damp cloth to rinse. Don't get him too wet, or you could damage the filling and/or have problems with mildew (and that would be another email to me!). Allow to dry naturally, or use a hairdryer on a low setting, gently teasing to fluff up the pile. If he's a bit smelly, freshen him up by sprinkling bicarbonate of soda over his surface, then rub in gently and leave for at least an hour before vacuuming with an upholstery nozzle.

Q **My cotton hat is meant to be waterproof, but I have additionally Scotchguarded it and it's pretty good. The problem is, it smells! I've had it four years, and it's acquired a rather 'unwashed old man' odour. What can I do?**

A I know the smell – horrid. Lightly sponge the lining and band with a warm detergent solution to freshen up. Use the stuff for washing woollens, but don't submerge in water. Work up a lather with a sponge, then rinse off with a clean damp cloth, taking care not to get the hat too wet. Stuff the crown with kitchen paper to prevent shrinkage, and allow to dry naturally away from direct heat. If the band is leather, use saddle soap such as Punch Saddle Soap spray, from Timpson and other shoe repair outlets (or call 01604 646426 for stockists). Spray a small amount on to a soft cloth, work into the leather and wipe away residue. Buff and allow to dry.

If the outside needs freshening up, hold over a boiling kettle (wear oven gloves for protection) and allow the steam to penetrate the fabric for a few seconds before lightly brushing with a clothes brush. When it's clean, re-proof with your protector.

Q My Panama hat, a gift from Ecuador, is no longer the crisp, elegant headgear it once was. It got wet a few times and its final humiliation was being sat upon by my granddaughter on a car journey. Plus it's stained. Have I any hope in restoring it?

A Tut, tut, you should not have worn it in the rain (never mind allow it to be used as a cushion)! Once the shape and body are gone, they can be hard to restore.

Let's deal with the stains first. Dab with sticky tape, or gently rub with a clean eraser. For greasy stains, blot with a little lemon juice and rinse with a damp cloth. If you have no luck, lightly sponge the surface with a solution of 1 teaspoon gentle detergent for washing woollens to 300ml warm water, taking care not to over-wet. Rinse well with a damp cloth and air-dry.

Now for the shape. Stuff the crown with tissue and hold the hat over a steaming kettle (don't burn your fingers!), then work it back into shape with your hands. Keep steaming and shaping until most of the wrinkles are gone. Allow to air-dry. Still looking a bit limp? Lightly spray with hairspray. Now take care of it: avoid pinching the front and keep straw fibres pliable by lightly mist-spraying with water twice a year (beginning and end of summer), but don't wear in the rain. Store upside down (not on its brim) in a cool cupboard away from damp and direct heat, ideally in a hatbox. And don't store a foldable Panama rolled up!

Q I've stupidly splashed baby oil on my newly painted bedroom wall. The stain covers an area of about 2ft long by 6in wide and the oil has soaked right into the plaster. How can I remove the mark?

A Short of digging out the stained plaster and having it redone, you won't be able to get rid of the stain. But there is another way. Wash down the surface with warm soapy water and seal the area with Polycell Stain Stop (1 litre is enough to treat 9 sq m). This dries to form a barrier between the stain and the new paint and will stop the oil bleeding through. (If you don't seal the stain the oil will emerge, no matter how many layers of paint you use.) Apply with a paintbrush, making sure you treat an area slightly larger than the stain. When dry, repaint the whole wall.

Q How can I remove a (very annoying) stain on newly hung light-coloured wallpaper?

A If it's a grease mark, place clean kitchen paper over the top and press with a warm, dry iron to draw out the oiliness. Deal with any remainder by dusting the area with talcum powder before brushing off with a soft brush. You should be able to remove other marks by rubbing with a clean soft eraser or, strange as it sounds, a piece of stale bread.

Q How can I remove marks left by Blu-Tack on magnolia-painted walls?

A If it's relatively fresh and soft, the easiest way is with a fresh chunk of Blu-Tack. Dab it against the wall, removing a little at a time, otherwise you might damage the surface. If the Blu-Tack is hard, hold a plastic bottle filled with warm water over the area – it'll make it pliable again. Another idea is to rub the area with an ice cube, which makes the Blu-Tack brittle, allowing you to chip it off.

Occasionally, Blu-Tack will leave an oily stain. The makers suggest you use lighter fuel, but with extreme caution. Dip a tiny amount on cotton wool and dab, working around the oily area. The lighter fuel rehydrates the Blu-Tack so it can be removed. Any residue can be rubbed off with your finger.

Q My hairspray leaves a brown grungy build-up on the plates of the ceramic hair straighteners, which affects performance. It just won't scrub off – I can only scrape a

**little away when the straighteners are on. How can I get
rid of it properly?**

A Believe it or not, all you need is hot water and shampoo.
Shampoo removes the build-up of products in hair, so it'll have
the same effect on your straighteners.

Make sure they're cold (and unplugged) before you start,
then wipe over the plates with a damp cloth wrung out in the
shampoo solution. Rinse and allow to dry completely before
using again. The only way you'll stop this happening again is
to refrain from using hairspray until *after* you've straightened
your hair; you shouldn't be using it with the straighteners
anyway. Ideally you should use a heat protection spray instead.
Apply to wet hair, and then roughly blow-dry before running
the plates through sections of your hair. Finally, use your
beloved hairspray to set the style.

Q My house is for sale and I want to get a good price
without spending very much on it. I'd like to freshen up
the white laminate built-in bedroom furniture, which has
gone a bit grey. Cleaning has made no difference. Can
you help?

A You can scrub all you like but you won't restore the finish;
laminate discolours with age, particularly in direct sunlight.
Paint it instead (sounds a hassle, but you don't have to sand
the surface and it needs only one coat). Wash with warm,
soapy water, dry with a soft cloth and apply International
Quick-Drying Multi-Surface Primer. Then use International

One Coat Furniture & Cupboard Paint with Teflon. It comes in eight colours; available from DIY stores.

Q I have an old brass plate (about 1m diameter) coated in lacquer. Some lacquer has worn away and it's possible still to polish these exposed parts. However, the remaining lacquer is dirty and discoloured – how can I remove the old stuff so that I can polish the whole plate?

A Simple: with a proprietary paint and varnish remover, but make sure the room is well ventilated and you wear rubber gloves. Apply with a paintbrush and gently rub the surface with very fine steel wool, then wipe with a clean rag and water.

Now for cleaning the brass underneath: wash the plate in warm soapy water, brush gently with a soft brush, rinse and dry with a soft cloth. Then use either a proprietary metal polish or rub the surface with half a lemon dipped in salt. Rinse immediately (otherwise it could pit the surface) and buff dry with a soft cloth. To protect the plate from re-tarnishing, apply a couple of coats of Rustin's Clear Metal Lacquer, from hardware stores, or call 020 8450 4666.

Q My wardrobe is set against an outside wall and all my suede shoes have gone mouldy. How can I bring them back to life?

A Gently clean off the surface mould with a suede brush – do this outside so you don't breathe in any spores. If mould has penetrated and stained the suede, hold each shoe over a boiling kettle (wear oven gloves for protection) and allow the steam to penetrate the leather – the heat will kill the mould spores and stop them spreading. Use a suede brush to raise the nap and, when dry, clean with a suede shampoo to try to remove any staining. Always test on a less visible area (back of the heel), then allow to dry thoroughly, away from direct heat. And of course you'll have to deal with your damp wardrobe, otherwise you'll be right back where you started.

Law of window cleaning:

it's on the other side

_____

Anon

Outside

Q How can I clean an external brick wall discoloured by long-term overflows from a bathroom pipe? The stain is greenish, tinged black near ground level (where the hard surface is Tarmac).

A I imagine the overflow has encouraged algae to grow, and the black areas are where the algae is dying off. Fix the leak, then clean the wall with HG's aptly named Green Slime Remover (01206 795200; www.hg.eu). It does exactly what it says on the bottle and is good for removing mould, algae, lichen or moss from patios, paths, roofs, fences and terracotta pots, as well as brick walls. It's perfectly safe to use near your plants or grass but you must apply it in dry weather and when no rain is forecast for the next couple of days – not easy, I know. Dilute a quarter of a bottle with half a bucket of water and apply the solution with a watering can, broom, scrubbing brush or plant spray; there's no need to rinse off. The cleaner takes about 36 hours to remove the algae but penetrates deep into the surface and will protect against regrowth for several months.

Q At Hallowe'en someone threw eggs at houses in our street and I can't get the stain out of the brickwork. The bricks are soft, so I don't want to brush too hard.
A Once dried, egg is difficult to shift, so if you've not tried already, scrub with a stiff brush and warm soapy water. The secret is first to saturate the area with plain water, and then clean from the top down. Make sure you keep the brickwork below the area being cleaned wet, and rinse thoroughly with plenty of clean water. This will stop white scum forming and limit the amount of detergent and other loose particles being absorbed. Otherwise you could use a pressure washer on a *very* low setting, but take great care not to damage the bricks or the joints.

If this doesn't work, try Delphis Eco Masonry & Stone Cleaner, £3.45 for 750ml (0151 5301855; www.delphisworld. com). Made from natural and fruit-based materials, it's free from hazardous chemicals and acids, is safe around children and pets and won't harm the environment. Spray directly on to the surface, agitate with a wet brush, leave to stand for five minutes then rinse off with warm water. Heavy soiling may require a longer standing time. Bear in mind that whichever method you use, you'll probably end up with a lighter patch on the spot where you've cleaned (unless you clean the whole wall).

Q How can I get rid of the horrible green sticky stuff that's accumulated on the roof of my conservatory? I think it's from nearby trees. No joy from my pressure washer.

A Your pressure washer is a good idea, but you need something with more welly to cut through the stickiness, such as a rotary wash-brush accessory to go on the end of the washer. Most manufacturers do them; for example B&Q sells the MacAllister Rotary Wash Brush, £19.98 (0845 6096688; www.diy.com), which comes with adaptors to suit most makes of electrical pressure washers. It's like a giant washing-up brush with soft bristles, so is safe to use on glass; the rotary action will get rid of the dirt. I'd also use proper pressure washer detergent: something like Kärcher Wash & Wax (to prevent streakiness), £8.81 for 5 litres from Tesco Direct (0845 6004411; www.tesco.com). Rinse and allow to dry.

Once cleaned, think about treating the roof with Clear-Vision Windows & Glass Furniture Kit from Ritec (0845 2304888, www.clearshield.biz), £56.23 inc p&p. It's not cheap and a bit of a faff, but forms an invisible barrier to help repel dirt, and should last up to two years. It includes a protector that chemically bonds to the glass and repels water, which means you shouldn't have to clean the glass so often, and when you do, it'll be easier. The kit has all you need for a three- to four-bedroom house, so there will be plenty for your conservatory.

Q My conservatory has a particularly high roof and it's difficult to clean the glass. Are there any methods you could suggest so that I can reach it more easily?

A Try a pressure washer, such as the Kärcher K399M, around £150 from DIY stores. It attaches to a standard garden hose and comes with a 6-m high-pressure hose. For ease, you'll need the Rotary Wash Brush (around £29.99) and the Vario 4 Extension Lance (around £44.99). The brush can be angled for tricky areas and the rotary action removes dirt and algae. The extension lance can be adjusted up to 1.7m so you should be able to clean the roof without a ladder. Use Kärcher's Wash & Wax detergent to prevent streakiness, £8.81 for 5 litres from Tesco Direct (0845 6004411; www.tesco.com). Rinse and allow to dry.

For a cheaper option, try the Leifheit Window Cleaning Mop, £14.67 from Lakeland (01539 488100; www.lakeland.co.uk). It has a telescopic handle that extends up to two metres, and a squeegee swivel head with a microfibre fleece, which slips off easily for cleaning.

Once the glass is clean, apply Clear-Vision Windows & Glass Furniture Kit from Ritec (0845 230 4888; www.clearshield.biz; £56.23 inc p&p) to the exterior. The kit includes a protector that helps to repel dirt. This should mean you won't have to clean so often, and when you do, it'll be easier. It should last up to two years.

Q We live on the sixth floor of a Victorian mansion building with double-glazed sash windows, the outsides of
which are impossible to wash. Someone told me about
magnetic cleaners but I've not come across them. Can
you help?

A Wintecs Window Cleaning Supplies (0844 8842606;
www.wintecs.co.uk) sells the Window Wizard Magnetic
Squeegee: single glazed, £22.45 (for glazing up to 12mm
thick); and double, £27.59 (for glazing up to 24mm) inc p&p.
Buy the right one for the glass thickness because if the magnet
is too strong, it'll be difficult to move.

The kit comprises two units, both of which have a built-in
magnet, washing sponge and rubber squeegee for drying. The
outer unit has a safety cord to guard against dropping. To use:
dip the units into warm soapy water (for good drying results
use a weaker solution than recommended, and squeeze out
the excess), then attach the unit with the cord on the outside,
the other inside, sponge to sponge and blade to blade. Move
from side to side, in the direction of the arrow, working from
top to bottom and finishing at a corner. They do a reasonable
job – you might have a few smears, and it's difficult to get into
the corners or to use on small multi-paned windows, but for
you they will be better than nothing.

Q How can I remove black permanent marker pen from
glass? Some imps have run along the length of one side
of our car windows, and we can't get it off.

A Buy the finest grade wire wool from the hardware shop, dampen it and go at the pen marks. And no, it won't scratch the glass.

Q How can we remove engine oil that has leaked on to our block-paved driveway?
A Try Lithofin Oil-Ex, £18.68 inc p&p for a 250-ml tube from Extensive (0845 2261488; www.extensive.co.uk). This works like a poultice, drawing out the stain, but must only be used in dry and warm conditions (over 10°C). Apply generously with a stiff brush and leave eight to 14 hours. Once dry, brush off the resultant powder and rinse with water. Deeply ingrained stains may need more applications.

Q I have a slippery York stone driveway. I can remove the moss with an electric power jet hose, but there are still black patches that won't budge. Any ideas?
A In deep shade, damp, hard surfaces are prone to moss, lichen and algae, especially in winter and spring. And it's worse if the driveway doesn't have an adequate slope to allow the water to drain away. I'm surprised, though, that your pressure washer hasn't removed the black patches (where the moss has discoloured the stone). Here are some remedies.

For a quick fix, try these steps:
✳ Scrub the drive with a stiff brush, using a mixture of sharp sand and water.
✳ Use a patio and drive cleaner, such as Jeyes Path, Patio &

Drive Cleaner, from garden centres and DIY stores, or call 01842 757575 for stockists. Or Lithofin Outdoor Cleaner, £17.78 per litre, including p&p; enough to treat 5–10 sq m; from Extensive (0845 2261488; www.extensive.co.uk). These are usually best applied with a watering can and rose. Scrub with a stiff brush, leave for the specified time and rinse well.

✳ Add a detergent to your pressure washer. Try Kärcher Patio & Deck Wash, from DIY stores or call 01295 752200 for stockists. Add the detergent to your machine (via the detergent suction tube or tank, depending on your washer) and spray the drive using a low-pressure setting. Leave it to work for five to 10 minutes, then rinse with plain water on high pressure.

But these steps won't stop the moss returning. For a longer-term solution, use a proprietary algae and moss remover such as Lithofin Algex, £20.20 per litre, inc p&p; enough for about 10 sq m (after using the Outdoor Cleaner as above), also from Extensive. This will not only clean and kill the moss but will also prevent regrowth for up to a year. However, it may take up to a few weeks for the discoloration to disappear. Best done in dry weather: dilute one part Algex to 10 parts water and apply with a garden sprayer or watering can with a rose spray. Leave and allow the rain to wash it away. In badly soiled areas, repeat, using a stiff brush.

Q I sprayed our side of the neighbour's new fence with Cuprinol Sprayable Fence Treatment, and the wind blew it on to his sandstone patio, which now has a fine covering of brown. I've jet-washed and scrubbed it to no avail. Help!

A Shame it wasn't hosed off while still wet, but no worries, the technical guys at Cuprinol say, because it's a water-based product, you should still be able to remove it. Don those wellies and rubber gloves, fill a bucket with very hot soapy water – that's the key here – and give the area a really good scrub with a stiff yard brush. Rinse thoroughly afterwards.

Q I have a coconut-fibre front doormat that fits into a well for which it was made when the house was built in the early 1960s. It's still in good condition but very dirty. How can I get it clean again? We have a Kew jet hose cleaner but I hesitate to use that as it may be too fierce.

A If it's a standard coir doormat (as opposed to seagrass, which must be dry cleaned), it's simple: take it outside on a sunny day, turn upside down and give it a bash with a broom, then flip over and vacuum. Repeat until you've removed as much loose dirt as possible, then put on your wellies and give it a good scrub with a stiff brush and a bucket of warm soapy water. Rinse with the garden hose (yes, your jet hose cleaner may be too fierce) and allow to dry before putting back into the well. And don't leave it another 50 years!

Q Can I paint a brown-grained uPVC door white and, if so, what paint should I use? (This is no longer an outside door, as a porch door has been fitted.) The brown door was expensive and I can't justify replacing it.

A First clean and dry the surface (remove stubborn stains with a non-abrasive, solvent-free cream cleaner; check the product on a small area before you begin). Once cleaned, prime using International uPVC Primer. After four hours, you can over-coat the door with any paint, but for extra durability, I would suggest using International's 10 Year Exterior Gloss or Satin, which resists cracking and peeling. It comes in 11 colours including white, and is touch-dry in three hours. All products are available from DIY stores.

Q During the winter I left my teak garden table and chairs outside, protected by a waterproof cover. When I took the cover off, the furniture was covered in thick, black mould. I tried scrubbing with warm soapy water but this has removed only a little of the mould. What else can I do? They are about four years old and were painted with tung oil when new.

A You're going to have to sand right back to the wood. Sanding is hard work, and teak is tough, so use an electric sander to make the job easier. (For fiddly bits in between slats, sand by hand.) Start with coarse-grade sandpaper, follow with a medium grade and finish off with a fine-grade paper. Once you're back to the wood, wipe down with white spirit to remove dust. Finally, treat with a light coating of teak oil, such as Cuprinol Garden Furniture Teak Oil (call 0870 4441111 or visit www.cuprinol.co.uk for stockists). You can use tung oil, but this has a thicker consistency and tends to sit on the surface; indeed, this may have encouraged the mould to grow in the first place, especially if you'd oiled the furniture just before storing.

To prevent the mould coming back during winter storage, make sure you leave plenty of ventilation around the furniture when you wrap it up in the waterproof covers. To be honest, you don't need the covers; the furniture will be perfectly okay left to the elements. Then in the spring, when you come to get the furniture out again, give it a light sand (no need to do the major sanding as described above) and treat it with a coat of teak oil. Never oil the furniture when you're about to put it away for storage as this will encourage mould to grow. If, however, you prefer the weathered look, just scrub down with warm soapy water and rinse to clear any dirt, moss or algae.

Q **We have a bog-standard, non-electric retractable awning in striped canvas. The 4–5-in edge is left exposed when the awning is retracted and gets very dirty, with mould in places. How do I clean it?**
A Most awning manufacturers recommend using soapflakes dissolved in warm water – anything stronger could damage the fabric. As for replacing it, you'll have to go back to the original supplier. No one seems to supply covers since most

awnings are now fully retractable, so you should remove the valance if possible during winter (usually by unscrewing and sliding out). If the soapy water doesn't do it, then you have nothing to lose by using a bit of Milton, followed by a tent-cleaning product.

Start by vacuuming off any loose dirt and mould spores, then sponge over a diluted solution of Milton Sterilising Fluid (1 tablespoon per litre of warm water). Follow with a tent-cleaning product such as Nikwax Tech Wash, around £10.99 per litre. Dilute in warm water and work up a lather with a sponge. Rinse thoroughly. Finish off while still damp with a waterproofer such as Nikwax Tent & Gear Solarproof, around £6.99 for 500ml, suitable for synthetic fabric (most awnings are), to help repel stains and mould as well as protect colours from fading. Allow to air-dry completely before retracting. For stockists, call 01892 786400 or visit www.nikwax.com.

Sounds like too much faff? Contact Awning Cleaning (020 8464 2517; www.awningcleaning.co.uk). Unfortunately it currently operates only in London and the Home Counties and charges £172.50 for the first awning, then £57.50 there-after. You should clean your awning every two or three years to prevent the build-up of dirt and help prolong its life.

Q Our cream sailcloth outdoor umbrella has become discoloured and spotted. How can I clean and re-proof it?
A The spots are probably mould, especially if you put it away last autumn while damp (you know you did). You need to

erect the umbrella and vacuum off any loose dirt and mould spores, which should remove surface staining. Then sponge over a diluted solution of Milton Sterilising Fluid (1 table-spoon per litre of warm water).

Follow up with a tent-cleaning product such as Nikwax Tech Wash, around £10.99 per litre. Dilute in warm water and work up a lather with a sponge. Rinse thoroughly. Finally, finish off while still damp with a waterproofer such as Nikwax Cotton Proof, around £13.99 per litre or, for synthetics, Nikwax Tent & Gear Solarproof, around £6.99 for 500ml. For stockists, contact 01892 786400 or visit www.nikwax.com. But this will make the umbrella only showerproof (not completely waterproof) on account of the open weave. And this autumn, dry completely before packing and storing away!

Q **I have a heavy metal garden table with an intricately moulded top, which is dirty with the usual outdoor grime. Some years ago, when it was in a similar parlous state, I had it sandblasted and spray-painted. How can I avoid the expense of another sandblasting and painting (without having to spend hours going at it with bleach and a toothbrush)?**

A If it's superficial, you should be able to clean it with a pres-sure washer on a medium setting – great for getting into nooks and crannies with little effort, but always test on a hidden area first (say, underneath the table or on a leg). If that fails, you're back to scrubbing down with hot soapy water

> ### TOP TIP
>
> #### *How to clean a rusty barbecue...*
>
> Scrunch up a handful of tin foil and rub, rub, rub to get the worst off, then wash with hot soapy water and a metal pot scourer.

and that toothbrush – or have it sandblasted again. It may be worthwhile checking with the local blacksmith if they can do it, alternatively contact the Leisure & Outdoor Furniture Association (01243 839593; www.lofa.com) for companies who can do this. As you know, it involves stripping the old paint back to the bare metal and repainting with a special coating to protect against weather and rust. Whatever you decide, there's no getting away from the fact that you need to give it a good going over with warm soapy water at the beginning of every summer.

Q Our brown uPVC window frames have paint, plaster and other debris embedded in the grain of the plastic. I've tried soap, water, elbow grease and various products without success and now the frames look old and tatty. Any ideas?
A Try rubbing with a proprietary cream cleaner such as Nilco uPVC Cleaner from Lakeland (01539 488100; www.lakeland.co.uk). You'll also need a modicum of elbow grease.

If more serious action is called for, use a plastic picnic knife or plastic ice scraper (the type for defrosting the freezer) and gently scrape away the deposits, taking extreme care to avoid deep scratches. Don't use a metal scraper as you'll wreck the surface. Once the paint and plaster are gone, go over the area again with the cream cleaner to help polish out any light scratching.

Stubborn stains and deep scratches will have to be dealt with professionally. This involves chemicals, special fillers and abrasive materials, but the surface can be polished back to look almost like new. The best place to start is to contact the supplier of your windows; most companies have a team of service engineers capable of doing repairs. If you inherited yours, look under 'Double Glazing Repair' in the *Yellow Pages*.

Q **My sports car's black fabric top has green, algae-like spots, probably because I have to park it under trees. I can't brush it very hard because it makes the surface 'furry'. I thought of using a dilute ammonia solution but am worried this might make the top blotchy. Any ideas?**
A Buy Autoglym Fabric Hood Cleaning Kit from Halfords or other car-accessory outlets. It's a two-part cleaning system that shifts general dirt, tree sap and algae, and protects the hood from water and soiling. Apply the cleaner to a damp roof and agitate with the sponge provided. Without letting it dry out, leave to work for a few minutes before rinsing off with clean water using a hose or watering can (not a pressure washer).

Remove excess moisture by patting the surface with a clean towel or chamois leather. Finally spray the roof with the protector, taking care not to get it on the windows or paintwork (if it accidentally runs down, quickly wipe away).

Q How can I get Sudocrem nappy rash cream off leather? My two-year-old had fun in the car, and I just can't shift it.
A The makers suggest you use a warm solution of washing-up liquid, but you need to be persistent because it's difficult to remove. Use an old soft toothbrush, particularly where the cream has worked into the grain of the leather, and wipe away with a soft cloth. Work in a gentle, circular motion, then rinse and repeat if necessary. And don't expect perfect results.

Q My husband uses chamois leathers for washing his car but after a while they get very grubby. The car wash shampoo doesn't cut it. Any other ideas?
A It's very hard to get rid of all the oil and grime, and eventually you have to chuck the leather and start anew. Meantime, after every use you should handwash the leather in a warm soapflake solution, squeezing to release the dirt (alas, Lux Soap Flakes are no longer around, but a good alternative is Dri-Pak Soap Flakes or Dri-Pak Pure Liquid Soap from supermarkets and hardware stores). Rinse in warm water to which you've added a teaspoon of olive oil (to keep the leather soft) and give it a quick swish. Squeeze hard and pull

into shape, then hang in an airy spot, away from direct heat, scrunching the leather once in a while to keep it supple. Store damp in a sealed jar.

Q At the end of last summer I lent my brother our family tent. Last week, I got it out and discovered it was flecked with mould and smelt musty. He clearly packed it away while damp. How can I remove the marks and smell?
A First get on the phone to your brother and tell him to make himself available next weekend. Don't stick the tent in the washing machine – there may not be enough space and the tent may have taped seams, which can become brittle after washing.

He'll have to erect it and vacuum off the mould spores, which should remove the surface staining. Then sponge over a diluted solution of Milton Sterilising Fluid (1 tablespoon per litre of warm water). And follow up with a tent-cleaning product such as Nikwax Tech Wash, around £10.99 per litre. You'll also need a waterproofer such as Nikwax Cotton Proof, around £13.99 per litre or, for synthetics, Nikwax Tent & Gear Solarproof, around £6.99 for 500ml – full instructions are on the packs. For stockists, contact 01892 786400 or visit www.nikwax.com.

Q We've just moved house and now have a septic tank. What would you recommend to keep it in good working order?

A As long as the tank has been installed correctly, it'll be fine on its own, without any bacterial additives. Follow these tips to keep your tank healthy.

✳ Generally speaking, you can use most household cleaners in moderation, provided they are used in accordance with the makers' instructions and stipulated concentrations, but don't use excessive amounts of detergent or bleach – it'll upset the natural balance of the system and cause it to smell.

✳ Never pour neat disinfectant or bleach down the sink or outside drains – they will kill the friendly bacteria that make the tank work. Always dilute well and use sparingly.

✳ Don't pour fats down the drain. Wash dishes in a dishwasher whenever possible (fat is converted into soap in a dishwasher).

✳ Nappies, sanitary items and condoms should not be disposed of into the system.

✳ Don't use the toilet or kitchen sink as a rubbish bin – never dispose of chemicals, pesticides, paints and the like into the tank.

✳ Have it inspected and emptied when necessary. How often depends on its size and frequency of use, but as a guide, call in the experts once or twice a year.

Q I've tried everything I can think of, but I can't get rid of unsightly red streaks of shoe polish on my vinyl bathroom floor. What can you suggest?

A I wonder what you're using because a little washing-up liquid and water should do it (always use a soft cloth, never a scourer, as you could remove the top layer of the floor and lose the sheen). If you've already tried that and have had no joy, dab a bit of white spirit on a cloth and rinse well.

Repairs

Q How can I disguise a chip on my cream-coloured laminate kitchen worktop?

A You need ColorFill by Unika Color Products (0191 2590033; www.unika.co.uk). There are over 300 shades, so you should find one to match. To make your search easier, call or use Unika's website database, which lists the main worktop manufacturers. If you know the product reference number, it can give you the closest match and stockist details. Otherwise, order by mail from Color Products (08456 585212; www.colorproducts.co.uk); £11.49 inc p&p (send an off-cut or end strip if possible).

To use, first remove any loose fragments and clean the area with the solvent supplied to remove any grease. Then apply the ColorFill using a metal spatula; leave to dry. The filler will sink as it dries, so repeat until level with the rest of the worktop. Clean off excess with the solvent between each application. Allow 24 hours to harden, then give a final clean with warm soapy water.

Q **My 16-month-old son has just scribbled all over my computer screen with a ballpoint pen. How can I get it off?**
A Depends on the screen. If it's the old glass type, you can safely use meths. Wipe a small amount over the glass, taking care not to get any on the plastic surround (swiftly wipe with a clean, damp cloth if you do). Buff dry with a clean, lint-free cloth. If, however, it's a plastic LCD flat screen, you must only use a special cleaner, such as IXOS XC14-F Screen Cleaning Wipes, from PC World (0844 5610000; www.pcworld.co.uk). Always check with your user manual first, in case the screen has a special coating, such as anti-glare. I'm not sure how successful you'll be, but avoid over-wetting the screen and take great care not to rub too hard, as you could damage the liquid-crystal cells behind the screen. But depending on how much pressure your little one used, the screen may have already sustained damage, rendering it illegible in parts. If this is the case, you'll need to replace the screen.

Q **Newish curtains in my house's large bay window 'stick' when drawn. They are hung from a shaped cord-operated metal Silent Gliss curtain track and for the first few months opened and closed easily, despite the weight of the fabric. Any advice?**

A You need Free 'n' Easy from Lakeland (01539 488100; www.lakeland.co.uk). This leaves a thin, invisible film to give effortless sliding, and can be used on curtain rails, drawers, doors, windows, patio doors, etc. One squirt lasts for months: apply a tiny amount along the track, then open and close the curtains a few times to work it in. Allow to dry thoroughly. It's silicone-based and odour-free, so won't stain the curtains.

Q I chipped a pretty single-flower glass vase and am searching for a glue that will leave a perfectly seamless join.
A Loctite Glass Bond, from DIY stores, dries clear when exposed to daylight and is suitable for gluing glass to glass (but not crystal) or glass to metal. It's water and detergent resistant (but not dishwasher-proof).

Q How can I remove scratches from a radiator with a high-gloss black finish?
A It's a repaint job. International Paints does a Heat Resistant Enamel (available in black only), which gives a tough, high-gloss finish, to withstand temperatures up to 200°C. First remove any flaking paint and ensure the surface is clean and dry. Apply paint with a natural bristle brush or a roller suitable for solvent-based paint. It'll be touch-dry in six hours and, if you need a second coat, apply after 24 hours. For other colours, use any emulsion and overcoat with International Radiator Clearcoat, which stops the emulsion peeling or discolouring. Both are available from DIY stores.

Q I have a glass-topped coffee table that's covered in fine scratches – none very deep, but the table looks unsightly. Is there anything I can do?

A There is, but it doesn't come cheap. Costs start at about £250 (plus travelling) so it might be better to replace the glass. If it's worth it, Reface Ltd (0845 3705888; www.reface.co.uk) offers a nationwide scratch-removal service for patio doors, conservatories and glass furniture. They sand the surface to remove the scratches, then re-polish to restore the sheen. Most scratches are superficial so there will be no real loss of strength or change in the fracture properties of the glass. However, if the glass sits in a frame, scratches right near the edge can't be treated without risking damage to the frame.

The process can be used on flat or curved glass, but not on textured glass or if there's a surface coating on the damaged side.

Q My new patent shoes are already marked – I think the sole of one foot rubs against the upper of the other as I walk. I've tried scraping at the marks with my nail (no success), but am afraid of breaking the surface with anything rougher. Any suggestions?

A Try sponging down with a mild solution of soapflakes – the stuff you get for washing delicates. Test a discreet area, say the back of the heel, and if you're happy, sponge the whole surface down (but don't over-wet). Rinse and pat dry before drying naturally away from direct heat. If you have no luck, try Punch Patent Glow from Timpson. Spray on, leave for a minute, then wipe with a soft cloth.

Q I wore my new cream silk kitten-heeled shoes to a wedding, but we had to walk across wet grass and the heels are now badly mud-stained. Is there anything I can do to (even partly) restore them to their former glory?

A Mix up a strongish solution of biological washing powder or liquid in hot (but not boiling) water and steep the heels in this for a couple of hours. Then take a soft toothbrush and gently work at the stains. Rinse, pat dry with a clean towel and leave to air-dry.

Q How can I remove scuff marks from a pair of (borrowed) ivory satin wedding shoes? They have senti-mental value for my friend, who lent them to my daughter when she got married.

A Without seeing them, it's difficult to advise, but try mixing up a fairly concentrated solution of soapflakes – the gentle stuff for washing woollens and delicates. Give it a good swish round to create lots of bubbles and use only the froth to clean the *whole* surface of the shoes (to minimise water marks). Test a less visible area first – say part of the heel. Rinse carefully by dabbing lightly with a barely damp white cloth wrung out in clean water and leave to air-dry away from direct heat.

The trouble with living alone is

that it's always your turn to do the dishes

Anon

Leave it to the experts

Q **My suede jacket has an ink mark – can I get this off myself?**

A Don't even try. Suede is very delicate and you might damage the finish and set the stain. No dry cleaner can guarantee to remove all stains but the Dry Cleaning Information Bureau (020 8863 8658, www.tsa-uk.org) can advise on local suede and leather specialists.

To keep your jacket looking good once it has been cleaned, apply a waterproof spray to protect against weather and stains – best done by the dry cleaner as they can make sure it's applied evenly. Then, as long as the jacket doesn't get too grubby, remove light surface soiling yourself by gently dabbing with a clean damp white cloth before hanging up to dry – but act quickly. (If the garment isn't re-proofed you'll need to have it cleaned professionally.) Never use a wire brush or suede block as you could end up with a lighter, bald patch.

Q How do I spruce up my beloved old white leather jacket, please?

A First, leather garments should never be washed. Get your jacket professionally cleaned by a reputable dry cleaner: contact the Dry Cleaning Information Bureau (020 8863 8658; www.tsa-uk.org) for members. After cleaning, it will be re-oiled to keep the leather supple and re-finished to restore the colour and protect against weather and stains. Then, as long as it does not get too grubby, you can remove surface marks yourself by gently rubbing with a soapy sponge (use a soapflake solution, never washing-up liquid). Wipe with a clean damp cloth and hang up to dry away from direct heat.

Q I used fake tan recently and must have spilt it on my beige carpet as it now has orange stains. What's the solution?

A Don't try treating it yourself. Call in a member of the National Carpet Cleaners Association (0116 2719550; www.ncca.co.uk). If they can't shift it, they can re-tuft small areas or replace a section of the carpet if you have off-cuts. Failing that, check your insurance policy to see if you're covered for accidental damage. In future, if the spillage is detected *before* it dries, immediately wash off with warm soapy water.

Q I've inherited an embroidered picture from my grand-mother, on canvas with silk and wool stitching. I'd love to clean it and revive the colours – any suggestions?

A Yes: leave it to the experts – it's just not worth the risk doing it yourself. Embroidered silks and wools are seldom colour-fast, plus you don't know how all the different fibres are going to react and it could shrink. Then there's the problem of how it's mounted (glues are often used).

I suggest you contact the Royal School of Needlework (020 31663932; www.royal-needlework.org.uk), which offers a restoration service. The people there will work on anything, from 300-year-old tapestries to everyday objects of sentimen-tal value. They can also do repairs, colour-matching and replacing individual stitches or re-weaving the canvas. Prices vary depending on the work done, but they'll give you an idea of cost before going ahead. Make an appointment to visit or send your embroidered picture by recorded post.

Once cleaned, hang your picture out of direct sunlight rather than tucking it away in a cupboard – it needs the air to circulate freely and prevent mould forming.

Q I have an antique quilt of great sentimental value (it belonged to my late mother). The stitching is starting to deteriorate, and it's showing its age. I've searched for specialist repairers, but can't find any. Can you help?

A I can recommend the Royal School of Needlework (020 31663932; www.royal-needlework.org.uk), who offer a restoration service. To start, the quilt will be cleaned, either in-house or by a specialist. Repairing it may include re-lining, re-stitching and re-embroidering. Threads and fabric are matched as closely as possible or can be dyed. Prices depend on the work, but they will talk through your options and give you an idea of cost beforehand.

Acknowledgements

Thank you, Gill Morgan, my long-time friend and editor of *The Times Magazine*, for asking me back in 2003 to have a go at a column. The first week's queries were made up, but thereafter have all been questions from *Times* readers, to whom I am also grateful.

Thanks to Kate Adams who commissioned the book (we'll miss you!) and to Bethan O'Connor who carefully nursed it through each stage; to my super agent Debbie Catchpole and her lovely assistant Verity O'Brien; and to The Plant for the cute illustrations. Biggest appreciation goes to my eminently efficient and persistent researcher Emma Burton, without whose help I would be unable to continue the column.

Index

Index